GREYHOUND RACING FOR PROFIT

CW00954243

Liam Connolly

ISB No. 0900611 41 3

RACEFORM LTD., COMPTON, NEWBURY, BERKSHIRE

FOREWORD

As I say in my autobiography *The Life and Secrets of a Professional Punter,* times are the be all and end all for the greyhound backer. I found the assistance of a time expert who had learnt his trade in greyhound racing invaluable when assessing time in horse racing. The student of time related to form is much better off in greyhound racing, where all the races are timed electrically.

I have always been surprised that there is not a basic book on greyhound racing which explains how to use times to find winners at the greyhound track, but I must congratulate Liam Connolly for being the first to write such a book. He also shows very clearly how to relate *time* to *class*, another of the main clues to finding winners.

Many people can find winners, but the difference between the fitted amateur and the true professional is, as I have always argued, getting value for money. Liam Connolly's book shows you how to do this, and after reading Chapter 6, *Betting Strategy*, I looked through the reports of the betting market at selected greyhound tracks. In some cases, you can get very good value indeed, and at least as good as the best horse racecourses.

It is some time since I have been greyhound racing regularly, but I can still remember the early days of walking away from the track with a pocket full of white fivers. For the newcomer or the enthusiast, Liam Connolly's book is an invaluable aid to finding winners.

ALEX BIRD

CHAPTER ONE

Greyhounds - The Best Bet

Greyhound racing, the second most popular spectator sport in Britain, has taken on a new lease of life in the last two or three years. Attendances at most tracks are up, Tote records are broken almost every year, and a whole new set of followers has been won to the sport through the screening of daytime races in the betting shops via the Satellite Information Services. The extent of public interest can be gauged by the fact that in 1988 £40 million was wagered in the betting shops on racing at Hackney.

As a spectacle, greyhound racing is hard to beat. Even at a big circuit, such as Hackney or Wembley, it is difficult to get more than about 120 yards away from the racing - whereas on the straight Flat courses, such as Newmarket, the horses begin at least 2000 yards away in some races. Even the racecourse commentator using a telescope has to waffle for the first 200 yards before he can make any sensible comments about the runners' progress.

Race reading is much easier, as the colours are standardised as follows for every race :

Trap 1 Red

Trap 2 Blue

Trap 3 White

Trap 4 Black

Trap 5 Orange or yellow

Trap 6 Black and white stripes

There are far more close finishes in greyhound racing, and the kind of race seen fairly often in two year old or all-aged plates or steeplechases with small fields - one horse coming home well clear with the others strung out so far behind that the result is a foregone conclusion with a furlong still to 'race' - is rarely seen in greyhound racing.

Much of the support for the 'sport of kings' and prejudice against greyhound racing - summed up in the phrase 'going to the dogs' - is based on sheer snobbery. Go and see for yourself - a greyhound card is all action with races every 17 or 18 minutes, and an exciting finish in almost every race.

The prejudice was certainly nourished by the Turf establishment from the early days of the sport. Before the end of its first year (1926) up to 30,000 spectators flocked to the meetings at Belle Vue, Manchester. As far as the they were concerned, horse racing simply could not compete.

Attendances at all live sporting events are down from the halcyon days of the late '40s and early '50s, but greyhound racing has maintained its relative position. It has survived some difficult years without the lavish subsidy received by horse racing - a most unjust situation given the millions of pounds made by off-course bookmakers from betting on greyhounds yet who put very little back into the sport.

Like many others, I was converted to the sport by the unforgettable Scurlogue Champ, seeing that unbelievable flying finish produced race after race. But what gave me a long-term interest after the Champ had retired was seeing the other races - the close, contested finish, with the result in doubt right up to the line which is the rule rather than the exception in greyhound racing.

One of the difficulties in evaluating horse racing form is that many races are not truly contested. Seeing so many hard fought finishes in greyhound races made me wonder whether they might not offer more opportunities. **I soon realised that from a betting point of view greyhound racing has no equal.**

A few simple points of comparison with horse racing will make it clear why there are many more good betting opportunities at the greyhound track.

Firstly, the sheer **quantity** of form is much greater. If you are interested in 6f handicaps for three year olds and upwards, at Newmarket there are usually 11 of these races in the 8 months Flat season. Over the same period at, say, Hackney, counting only the higher grade races (roughly comparable to the 0-90 handicaps upwards on the Flat) there are at least 150.

In the Flat racing season, the astute backer will confine his operations to the period between Royal Ascot and the Ayr Western meeting (14 weeks). During the winter, only the 8 weeks before Christmas can usually be counted on to offer reliable form lines. In greyhound racing, there are at least 24 weeks (from April to September) in every year when there is good form. In most years, you can expect 36 weeks; and sometimes, you can bet throughout the year.

The **quality** of form is not comparable. Two of the major factors in weighing up horse race form - ability to act on the course, suitability to the distance - usually do not come into the reckoning. In most races, the graded races (comparable to handicaps), the dogs are racing on the same track week in, week out, over the same distance. All tracks are left handed. Even the going is rarely a factor except in winter, because on sand tracks going variations are minimal even in wet summers.

Nor are you likely to be caught out by the 'dark horse' - the two year old running first time out, or the three year old running in plates without showing much, which then runs in a handicap.

Rule 48 of the NGRC (National Greyhound Racing Club) , which reads : 'A Greyhound to run in its first Graded Race at a particular Racecourse shall run at least 3 Initial Trials at that Racecourse on separate Days...' , is the major reason why there is no greyhound equivalent of the 'dark horse' under those circumstances.

If a dog 'finds' a great deal of time compared to his trial times, then the stewards are entitled to ask why - and frequently do so. At the major tracks, there are facilities for drug testing which have generally eliminated this danger.

If you confine your interest to the major tracks which run under the license of the NGRC, then you can be certain that greyhound racing is run in as straight a manner as possible, given the large amounts of money involved. The non-NGRC tracks are not quite so tightly controlled, and in any case offer a much lower standard of racing.

Secondly, greyhound form is much easier to assess because there is an **objective** source of information - race times. All races are electrically timed, whereas less than half (15 out of 35) Flat courses have electric timing. The time allowances made for changes in going are much more reliable than they are on the Flat. Despite the efforts of some highly talented time experts, I am unconvinced that it is possible to make suitable adjustments of recorded times in Flat races to allow for soft or heavy going.

A further indication of the importance of race times in greyhound racing is given by the fact that the record times are usually held by high class animals. A look at the list of record times on the Flat shows that many of the records are held by rather moderate animals, which won under unusual conditions, such as very hard going, or a strong following wind. **A record-breaking dog can be followed with confidence, whereas the same cannot be said of a horse.**

Not only does greyhound racing have accurate and reliable times for the race as a whole, but sectional times (to the winning post first time round) are usually calculated. It is true that these are nowhere near as fully calculated as in the U.S.A. - where the times to the first, second, third, and fourth bends are recorded on many tracks.

But not even the best equipped racecourses in this country have any means of timing, say, the first two furlongs of even the most important races. Any form expert will tell you that 'pace makes the race' - if the first two furlongs of a race of seven furlongs and over are run at a slow pace, the result can be very misleading.

It has never ceased to amaze me that so many horse racing fans and a section of the racing press are so keen on Flat racing times and even those for National Hunt - whereas relatively little attention is shown in the press to the structure and meaning of 'time form' in greyhound racing. If you don't read any other chapter in my book, at least read chapter 3 which analyses this crucial question.

Thirdly, more information about the animals is available. At the tracks, the racecards usually give the greyhound's weight on each of its previous appearances - not every racehorse trainer weighs his animals and none publishes this information in any systematic fashion.

In the racing press, the year and the month of a dog's birth is given - more precise information than is given in horse racing. A 'two year old' racehorse may be 2 years precisely or 2 years 4 months - quite a difference at this stage of his career. This information is available but is not easy to find.

Finally, while we have much more information about the animals themselves, the human factor does not intrude so much. You don't have to consider whether a dog has been badly ridden or will be better ridden next time. Nor do you have to wonder whether his trainer has placed his dogs in the right race : this is decided by the racecourse management. At the level of graded racing, most trainers are very capable. They all have their winning and their losing periods, but nowhere to the same extent as racing stables.

In recent years, the number of greyhound races at a given track has increased quite significantly, so that in effect the dogs do most of their training on the track. This may have diminished the art of the trainer, but it is a plus for the backer, as it means that if a dog runs regularly it is almost certain to be fit.

Many new punters, particularly those who are interested in horse racing, find it difficult to understand the basics of greyhound racing. These are explained in Chapter 2. If you are already a greyhound fan you can skip this chapter, but I hope that all types of readers will find something of value in the rest of the book.

CHAPTER TWO
The Racecard

Not only is greyhound form more reliable, but studying form is much easier as nearly all the information you require is given on the racecard. Full racecards are given in the sporting press for all the BAGS meetings (Bookmakers Afternoon Greyhound Service) and the evening meetings at the major tracks.

Because it contains a considerable amount of information, a greyhound racecard looks rather baffling to the beginner. Here is a typical, but imaginary card from Hackney.

12.24 (484 metres A1) £55

Trap 1 ORFORDS DOG w d Mendel - Silky Coat 10/84 Smith

29 Apr 484 1 3.86 2nd 2 Grey Racer e p 30.08 N 2-1F A1 30.24

Trap 2 GREY RACER bd d Fast Runner - Greyness 8/86 Brown

29 Apr 484 2 3.95 1st 2 Orfords Dog cwd 1 30.08 N 4-1 30.08

Trap 3 PERCY'S BOY f d Speed - Fast Finisher 9/85 Yeales

22 Apr 484 3 4.05 1st 4 Sloth fin well 30.00 - 10 5-1 A1 29.90

Trap 4 SLOTH be d Lazy - Slug 6/86 Robinson

22 Apr 484 4 3.90 2nd 4 Velocitas b blkd 1 30.00 - 10 7-2 A1 30.22

Trap 5 TOMMY (W) bd d Pater - Liza 5/85 Porter

27 Apr 484 6 4.08 5th 8 Win Easy ev ch 29.80 N 9-2 A1 30.44

Trap 6 DIANAS DREAM (W) bk b Rover - Delight 8/85 (Ssn 7/12/86) McCleary

15 Apr 484 5 4.00 1st 2 Canis al led 30.01 +20 6-1 3DT 30.21

Here is the explanation line by line of anything not immediately obvious.

The first line gives the details of the race.

A1 the distance and grade of the race. 'A' races are middle distance (for example, 484 metres at Hackney; 462 metres at Monmore Green); 'M' are an intermediate distance (523 metres at Hackney, confusingly, 484 metres at Monmore Green); and 'S' are long distance (670 metres at Bristol).

'1' means the top grade. At most tracks, the grades run from '8', the lowest, to '1', the highest.

Other common prefixes are : 'P' denotes races confined to puppies (bitches and dogs under 2 years old) ; 'OR' denotes 'Open Race'; 'IT' denotes 'Inter-Track'; and 'KS' Kennel Sweepstakes.

The remaining lines give the information about each competitor.

On the same line as Trap 1, we read the following :

w d white dog ('bd' - brindled; 'be' - blue, ie blue-grey; 'bk' - black).

In Traps 5 and 6, 'W' appears in brackets after the name - this means that

TOMMY and DIANAS DREAM have a tendency to run wide, and in order to make a fair race, they have been allocated to the outside traps.

In Trap 6 is the only bitch, marked by 'b'. After her birth date is given the date in which she last came into season ('Ssn') - if this information is not to hand, you will see 'n/s/d'; or if it has been suppressed by the vet, 'Ssn suppressed'.

10/84 date of birth.

Smith the trainer's name.

Next come the form lines (usually of the last 3 or 4 races, but here I have included only one, for the sake of simplicity).

The previous race was on 29 April over 484 metres.

1 the number of the trap from which he ran.

3.86 sectional time (time to the winning post first time round) in seconds

2nd final position

2 Grey Racer 2 lengths behind the winner, GREY RACER. If the distance is a fraction of a length, the same abbreviations are used as in horse racing, ie 'hd' for head and so on.

e p his running style, here 'early pace' - other common abbreviations being - 'blk' -baulked; 'c.a.' - came again; 'ck' - checked; ' cwd' - crowded; 'ev ch' - every chance; 'q.a.' - quickly away; 'rls' - rails; 's.a.' - slowly away.

30.08 the time of the winner (GREY RACER) in seconds, before going allowances. As the going is normal, no adjustment is necessary in this case.

N 'normal' going. In the form line for PERCY'S BOY you will see '-10' ie the going was .10 slow; for DIANAS DREAM +20 fast - the allowances to be deducted from or added to the recorded time.

2-1F the S.P. ie 2-1 favourite.

A1 the distance and grade of the previous race. At this point on the line for DIANAS DREAM, you will see '3DT' ie 3 dog trial.

30.24 the calculated finishing time time. 2 lengths (the losing margin) is reckoned to be equal to 0.16 seconds, which is added to the time of the winner to give the calculated finishing time.

As you can see, there is a mass of information here - how can it be used to find winners?

CHAPTER THREE

Understanding Greyhound Form

My answer is : rely solely on a study of form. Form works out very well in greyhound racing. **All other things being equal, the greyhound is one of the most consistent racing animals, certainly more consistent than the racehorse.**

Form is the answer. Many punters follow favourites, second favourites, or some combination of the two. I can't see the logic to *any* of the systems based on favourites, as they bear no relation to the actual performances shown by the dogs on the track. If you back a favourite, you are not even necessarily backing what the majority of other punters think will win the race - more often than not, you are backing the dog which the bookmakers *think* most punters will want to back. As often as not, it is the bookmakers who determine the initial prices, not the punters. **The bookmakers do not simply respond to demand from the public, instead they control the prices much more than most people realise.**

The other most favoured type of system in greyhound racing is based on individual traps or combinations of traps. Sometimes it involves waiting until there is a long losing run of a particular trap, on the principle that that trap is 'due for its turn'; sometimes the opposite principle, that a trap is 'in form' is favoured.

Like all systems, the systems based on traps are based on something real - the fact that at most tracks certain traps, usually Traps 1 and 6, are favoured.

It is also true that under certain conditions, one or two particular traps may provide a string of winners. For example, in wet weather, the going may be much softer on the inside of the track, thus giving the wide runners in Traps 5 and 6 a substantial advantage.

In some races, the grader (handicapper), who is usually the Racing Manager, may find that he is forced to line up a field of 4 or 5 railers and 1 or 2 wide runners, or vice versa. When this happens the dog in Trap 6 or Trap 1 respectively can have a chance better than his bare form indicates.

But even the more favoured traps can show very long losing runs. A simple calculation will show this to be true. If there are, say, 1000 races a year at a particular track, and 25% of the winners come from a particular trap, then during the course of the year that trap will provide 250 winners. But looked at from another point of view, then in 750 races the runner from this trap will be a loser.

This is a very favourable hypothetical example. I do not know of any track at which one trap provides 25% of the winners - the most favourable at any track rarely provides more than 20%, giving 800 losers out of a 1000 races.

Therefore, even a favoured trap can set up a very long losing sequence. Betting on combinations of traps seems even more foolhardy. In addition to the disadvantages I have just explained, forecast bets operate very much in favour of the bookmakers. They have worked out a special formula to calculate the odds on such bets. Unless you have several Ph.D.s in mathematics don't try to understand what this formula means. But there are no prizes for guessing whether it works in favour of the bookie or the punter.

WHAT IS GREYHOUND FORM?

Horse racing fans new to greyhound racing are often misled by a false analogy. Let us begin with an obvious case. If in racing horse A beats horse B at level weights by 4 lengths in a 12f race, then if they meet again over the same course and distance at the same weights then A is clearly the form horse. If on the second occasion A now has to give B 7lbs because he is carrying a penalty for the first win, the form expert might still reckon that A is the form horse, because of the manner of his victory in the first race.

Form should be analysed in quite a different way in greyhound racing. **The key principle is that it should be analysed much more literally.** If two dogs have a clear run, and dog A beats dog B by two lengths, he has won by two lengths, and that's all there is to it. Unless B is a young bitch clearly improving by leaps and bounds, and A is an older dog, if they meet within a month, A will almost certainly beat B by the same margin.

If a horse wins by two lengths, quite often this *cannot* be interpreted literally - just look at the wide variety of phrases in the form book when you have a two lengths winner : 'ridden out', 'eased near finish', 'all out', 'won cleverly'. Of course, you can occasionally turn this to your advantage, but it is a highly subjective process. Because of the control exercised by the jockey, interpretation is the key to horse racing form - whereas the greyhound just runs as fast as he can to the winning post.

If you are watching a race and the dog appears to win impressively - don't rely on this. It's not an impressive win until you know what the recorded time is. This also applies to the placed dogs - those within about 4 lengths of the winner will have run on as fast as possible right to the end of the race. In horse racing, the placed horses are often eased well before the finish.

Race reading is crucial in horse racing - it is nowhere near so important in greyhound racing. Its importance is also at a different point in the race. Whereas in horse racing you have to try and judge what the finish of a race means - ie did the winner have a lot 'in hand'? were the placed horses ridden out to the finish or eased near home? - as in greyhound racing it is the start and the first bend which are the most important.

What happens at the start as the dogs leave the traps is usually recorded very accurately in the press reports, but I have found that what happens at the first bend is not always reported with the same degree of accuracy. You do need to be at the track to watch carefully how the dogs take the first bend - which dogs run toward the bend in a straight line from the traps? which attempt to cut inside? which are genuine railers? which run for the middle of the track? which run wide at the bends?

Greyhound form is based on time. Before analysing how it works, it is necessary to see what types of races are most suited to form analysis.

TYPES OF RACES

The two major types of races are graded races, and Open races.

Graded races are the equivalent of handicap racing on the Flat. At each track there is a racing manager, whose task it is to classify all the animals at the tracks into different categories of ability. In graded racing, he can also allocate the runners to different traps (Rule 76 (v)).

There is also a special kind of graded racing known as 'Kennel Sweepstakes' (abbreviated 'KS') in which there is a prize, competed for by means of heats and a final.

Open races are the equivalent of Group or listed races, competed for by the best dogs at the track and open to dogs from other tracks. In such races, the traps are drawn for (Rule 76 (iii)).

In addition, there are 3 other types of race.

Inter-Track races are not always of Open Race class, but involve competition between dogs of the same grade from different tracks.

Handicap races have the front trap a metre in front of the second, and so on to the backmarker, 10 or 12 metres away, the 'scratch' dog. These are popular in the north of England, but the only southern BAGS track to offer them is Crayford.

Hurdle races add variety to a programme of graded races, but are rarely included in the BAGS meetings.

In my experience, the best bets are to be found in graded racing, in the higher grades - I usually concentrate on the top three grades (A1 A3, M1-M3, or S1-S3). At the lowest grade (A8), you usually find new, untried dogs, or dogs which have failed in the higher grades. The lower grades, A7-A4, are rather like the poorer class handicaps in Flat racing - moderate or inconsistent animals, with the older dogs being stuck in their grade. Quite often these races will also include two or three new animals which have only run in trials. Consequently, such races are very difficult to weigh up, and the result is usually something of a lottery.

In the A3-A1 grades you find that there are good quality, reliable animals, and enough form to provide plenty of betting opportunities.

Unfortunately, at some of the tracks, notably Brough Park, Monmore Green and Oxford, only lower-grade racing is offered in the BAGS programme. The higher grade racing is understandably enough reserved for local patrons who visit the track to see evening racing. The situation is not static - Bristol offered more graded races in the 1988 BAGS season than it has done in previous seasons.

BAGS programmes usually do not feature Open Races. It is difficult to compare form from different tracks and different distances, far more so than in horse racing.

Although ordinary Open races are contested by good-class reliable animals, I find events of this kind very difficult to weigh up. Form from different tracks and different distances is very hard to evaluate. But Open races run in heats are quite a different matter- by the time the dogs reach the semi-final or final, all the competitors have run recently at least twice over the course and distance.

Why do other types of race not, in my opinion, offer a reliable betting medium?

In theory, handicap races should give reasonable results, as the dogs do not crowd when the traps open and there is not so much bunching at the first bend. However, in practice, there are few opportunities in handicap racing, as there is little way of knowing what impact the concession of extra distance as a penalty for winning will have.

Hurdle races are difficult to assess, because there are relatively few of them and thus there is not enough form. Moderate flat racers often become outstanding hurdlers, but obviously their flat form gives no clue to their hurdling abilities.

Finally, avoid races with 8 runners. They offer more opportunities for complicated forecast bets, but even on a wide track like Monmore Green, the only BAGS track at which 8 runner races are currently held, there is more bunching. Winners are very hard to find in 8 dog racing.

How does the graded system work? Just as the handicap system in racing is based on weight, the graded racing system is based on time.

TIME AND GRADE

Every track has a racing manager (ie grader) whose job it is to sort the dogs at the track into different grades. To explain how graded racing works, look at it from the point of view of the racing manager. Let's take Hackney as an example, the principles being the same at all the tracks.

In order to be eligible to run in a race over 484 metres (the 'A' distance), a dog has to record a time of 31.00 secs or better. If he can do this, he is then 'graded in'.

If a dog achieves any time down to about 30.80, he runs in the lowest grade. At Hackney, this is the A8 grade. The remaining grades are determined by the times recorded by the dog, with the average time for each grade roughly as follows.

31.00 grading in ie A8

30.75 A7

30.60 A6

30.45 A5

30.30 A4

30.20 A3

30.05 A2

29.90 A1

The same principle applies over different distances. Thus over 523 metres ('M' at Hackney), the grading-in time is 33.30 seconds.

32.60 M3

32.40 M2

32.35 M1

(For the sake of simplicity, I have omitted the lower grades).

The times which the grader works to are not published. Although there does not seem to be any reason why they should not be published, just as in Flat racing the grade of the handicap is quite widely published, it is just a fact of racing life that they are not. The times given above are based on my own calculations, by taking the average time of 50 races at each grade.

Thus in a closely graded race, say an A2, the times of the competitors will range between about 30.40 and 30.15. That is, 0.25 seconds, which is equivalent to just over 3 lengths. The many close finishes which make greyhound racing such an exciting sport are a testimony to the consistency of the greyhound and a tribute to the ability of the grader.

The grader can penalise a dog which wins or runs close up in a fast time in several ways. He can raise him one or more grades; put him in a more difficult trap; or ask him to run against dogs with a different running style.

So if a dog wins, say, an A4 from Trap 1 in 30.55 seconds, the grader will probably keep him in the same grade; if in 30.45 seconds he may keep him in the same grade but in a more difficult trap, moving him 1 to, say, Trap 4; if in 30.30 seconds he will be upgraded to A3; if 30.20 perhaps Trap 4 in an A3.

The final possibility is that a dog may win an A4 in a moderate time, say 30.60, by showing early pace in a field of slow starters. It would be rather harsh to raise him to an A3 grade, so in his next race the grader will aim to put him in another A4 race, but in a line up of fast starters. The same principle, in reverse, would apply to a dog winning by a late challenge in a field of fast starters.

The grader's task is, therefore, in principle quite simple. But the right kind of dogs may not always be available. For example, suppose he has to make up 2 A3 races. Although there may be around 50 dogs in the track's kennels which have run in this grade, they will not all be available at any one time - some of the bitches will be in season, some dogs off colour, and so on. So making up a race of 4 relatively fast starters to test a dog rising from A4 grade may not always be easy.

Clearly, he is in a different position from the handicapper. The latter has a difficult judgement to make in assessing the value of a win, in terms of allocating weights for the future; but once that is done, he is not concerned with the make-up of future races.

Because the basic decision is relatively simple (unlike that of the handicapper), the grader is unlikely to make mistakes. Most races are closely graded; but where the grader does not have the range of choice he would like, he is obliged to produce a less closely graded race. In 9 races out of 10, the grader will be able to produce an 'ideal' line - up; but in the 10th race, circumstances force him to allow perhaps one or two dogs on favourable terms. This is where the patient backer can find opportunities.

Sometimes, I suspect, the policy of the racing management of a particular track is to re-grade a dog very lightly, and put him in his favourite trap. This is an obvious chance for the punter, and keeps him in a good humour. If you follow the racing closely at a particular track, you will soon see whether or not this happens with any regularity. When it does, be prepared to take advantage, although you are unlikely to be able to get a favourable price, as your choice will be equally obvious to everyone else.

Two qualifications need to be made to the general principles I have just outlined. The first is a minor one. The grades are roughly comparable at different tracks, with one exception. For no apparent reason Hove uses a different grading system, with the result that in my estimation an A5 there is the equivalent of at least an A3 anywhere else. (with A4 equal to A2, A3 to A1, and A2/A1 equivalent to some Open Races elsewhere).

Much more importantly, grading policy differs at various tracks. At some tracks, dogs winning in a reasonably good time are more severely punished than they would be at other tracks. To give an example, from a non-BAGS track, Wembley, winners in a reasonable time in the lower grade are often raised two grades, which seems to me rather punitive.

The Racing Manager has to work within the framework of policy set by the general management. Although there are guidelines for him to work along , it boils down to his subjective judgement. **Therefore it is important that you familiarise yourself with a particular track, and follow a limited** set of graded races (I suggest the top three grades) so that you know how the Racing Manager thinks, in order to be able to take advantage of his 'errors', deliberate and unintentional.

Once a dog has reached the top of the grading system, he is eligible for 'Open Races', This is the highest class of racing, in which dogs from other tracks than the 'home' track can compete. These are relatively open-ended in terms of time, right up to the track record (at Hackney, for example, this is 29.02 seconds).

MAKING A TIME INDEX

How can we use these times to work out greyhound form? Suppose there are three dogs, which have reliably recorded the following times in the A3 grade at Hackney.

Arthur   30.20

Bill   30.25

Charlie   30.18

With a closely grouped set of figures for one grade, like those above, the difference between the dogs' time figures are easy to see. However, when dealing with widely dispersed figures from different grades, the differences are more difficult to understand at a glance. For example, look at the following times recorded in different grades :

Dave   30.48 A4

Eddie   30.09 A2

Fred   30.26 A3

It is not easy, even with experience, to tell at a glance what each of these figures means. I find it essential to work with an index figure, say 100, which represents a time somewhere in the middle of the range of times for graded dogs.

I usually set this index figure at the average time for an A3 (or M3, for that distance) win. This is at a slightly higher point than the middle of the range of grades from A1 to A8. I do so because I am only interested in races from A3 upwards, and the location of the index figure should reflect this. If you are interested in *all* graded races, then you would have to locate your index at the average time of a much lower grade. It doesn't really matter as long as you stick to the index figure you have chosen!

At Hackney, the average time for an A3 win is 30.20 seconds. If we take this as our index figure of 100, we can now give the dogs in the first example (which is simpler, because only one grade is involved) the following index figures :

Arthur   30.20 = 100

Bill   30.35 = 85 ➡

Charlie   30.18 = 102

Bill's figure is .15 seconds *slower* than average, therefore, I *subtract* 15 ; Charlie's figure is .02 seconds *faster* than average, therefore I *add* 2.

Now if you look at the index figures alone, you can see the dogs' time figures at a glance :

Arthur   100

Bill   85 ➡

Charlie   102

This system is even more helpful when looking at dogs with times for different grades, as in the second example above. Re-cast using index figures, the times now look as follows :

Dave   72 A4

Eddie   111 A2

Fred   94 A3

Their relative abilities in different grades are now immediately apparent.

In order to calculate the index figure, you simply work out the average time (including going allowances) of at least 50 races for the A3 grade. To save the reader trouble, I include my figures for several leading tracks in Chapter 7.

If your local track is not included in that chapter, there is a short-cut to calculating the index figure. If you deduct .70 seconds from the grading-in time for the distance, and accept that figure as the 100 index figure, you will not be very wide of the mark.

Using this system of index figures, you can compile your own form book. In fact, not only *can* you, you *have* to, as there is no equivalent of the official Jockey Club form book, for graded races.

First the bare result.

Race 08* : 7 April 1988 HACKNEY M3 Normal 32.70

GREYHOUND	TRAP	PERFORMANCE	SECTIONAL	DISTANCE
Clipper Ship	2	rls, fin well	6.18	-
Oil Sheik	5	wide, fin well	6.20	1/2
Eamonn's Boy	6	q a led run in	5.98	1
Weekly Express	4	ran on	6.08	hd
Carlingford Boy	1	q a, led 1/2	5.99	hd
Coolruss Joy	3	ev ch	6.10	1

* the race number is purely arbitrary, given for future reference

Before working out the time index figures, try to recreate how the race was run. EAMONN'S BOY and CARLINGFORD BOY contested the lead from the first bend to the run in, where they were overtaken by CLIPPER SHIP and OIL SHEIK. The former's position on the rails at this point probably gave him the decisive advantage to run on to win.

There are no 'hard luck' stories - all the dogs had a clear round, and 3 lengths covers the entire field. Thus we can assume that this is a reliable result for the future. How do we calculate the time index?

14

*Race 08 : 7 April 1988 HACKNEY M3 Normal 32.70

GREYHOUND	TRAP	PERFORMANCE	SECTIONAL TIME		DISTANCE
Clipper Ship	2	rls, fin well	6.18		90
Oil Sheik	5	wide, fin well	6.20	1/2	86
Eamonn's Boy	6	q a led run in	5.98	1	78
Weekly Express	4	ran on	6.08	hd	77
Carlingford Boy	1	q a, led 1/2	5.99	hd	76
Coolruss Joy	3	ev ch	6.10	1	69

* indicates that I consider this a reliable result (see below)

Here we are interested in the figures in the column labelled 'Time'. The calculations may look slightly complex at first, but with a little practice, it takes less than 5 minutes to compile the whole table.

The winner's time of 32.70 is 0.10 seconds slower than the 100 index time for 'M' races (523 metres) at this track of 32.60., so he is given a figure of 90.

The figures for the others are adjusted according to the following table :

Less than a head = 0 points

A head = 1 point

1/4 length = 2 points

1/2 length = 4 points

3/4 length = 6 points

1 length = 8 points

This race was rather untypical - in most greyhound races, there is some more or less serious incident which spoils a dog's chances. How do we deal with this in compiling our time figures?

Race 16 : 21 April 1988 HACKNEY M3 +10 32.54*

GREYHOUND	TRAP	PERFORMANCE	SECTIONAL		DISTANCE
Three Speed	4	led 4 held on	6.08	-	
Wildcat Joe	3	led 1 to 4	6.02	1	
Ballylarkin Mini	6	handy from 3	6.11	hd	
Ballynaught Spot	1	ev ch	6.19	2	1/2
Star Exile	2	cwd 1	6.04	3/4	
Seldom Sober	5	ev ch	6.04	3/4	

* calculated time, adjusted for going allowance. Both figures are always shown in racecards, as well as the going allowance, but for the sake of clarity I only give the going allowance and the calculated time.

In our mental re-run of the race, STAR EXILE was crowded by WILDCAT

JOE at the first, and was unable to get back into the race; WILDCAT JOE led until the final bend, but was then overtaken by THREE SPEED, who held on to the finish. None of the others made an effective challenge.

Is this a reliable race? STAR EXILE did not have much of a chance on his previous form, so it is a reasonable assumption that his being out of contention after the first bend did not in fact materially affect the result.

How, then, do we assess the performance of STAR EXILE?

*Race 16 : 21 April 1988 HACKNEY M3 +10 32.54

GREYHOUND	TRAP	PERFORMANCE	SECTIONAL TIME		DISTANCE	
Three Speed	4	led 4 held on	6.08	-	106	
Wildcat Joe	3	led 1 to 4	6.02	1	98	
Ballylarkin Mini	6	handy from 3	6.11	hd	98	
Ballynaught Spot	1	ev ch	6.19	2	1/2	78
Star Exile	2	cwd 1	6.04	3/4	(72)	
Seldom Sober	5	ev ch	6.04	3/4	NR	

* indicates a reliable race

There are two new features in the column headed 'Time'.

Firstly, if a dog is baulked, bumped, checked, crowded, or hampered in any way, I put his index figure in brackets, as a sign that the figure does not represent a true performance. There is no point in either guessing what he might have done with a clear run or of discounting this run altogether - placing in brackets indicates that this is a conditional figure.

Secondly, I only compile the figures for dogs within 4 lengths of the winner, because my experience show that beyond this point time figures begin to lose their significance and are unreliable guides to future performance. These my dogs I mark on the index as 'NR' (abbreviation for 'not-rated').

Thus '(NR)' would mean that the dog was more than 4 lengths away from the winner, but this may not represent his true performance.

At this point, I must return to the distinction between a reliable and an unreliable race, to analyse it in more detail. This distinction is at the heart of my system, and explains why my figures often differ from those of other time experts in the press (eg *Clockwork* in *Sporting Life*).

To explain the distinction in more detail, consider the following types of races, which account for 9/10 of all races in which there are incidents.

1. Several dogs crowd at the first bend, including the form dogs, losing their chance at this point. A slow starter misses the melee, is left clear and runs on to win.

2. Most or all of the field emerges unscathed from the second bend, but there is crowding at the third or final bend, or on the run in.

3. The field crowds at most of the bends, and a slow starter, behind for most of the race, comes with a strong late run in the home straight to win almost on the line.

4. One dog goes off at a fast pace (shown by the sectional time) for this grade - the others are 'drawn along' fast to the first bend, where they all crowd. The leader gallops on strongly to win.

Of the four types of race, in which there are incidents during the race so that not all the competitors enjoy a clear run, only the last one gives a reliable result. In this type, under similar conditions (going and trap), you could reliably expect the winner to win again - in the other three types, you could not reliably expect either the winner or those involved in incidents to emerge the winner of a similar race.

Thus in my analysis of form, I only take into account as giving a clear, indisputable result race type 4; and the race in which all the dogs have a 'clear round'.

It is true that this restricts the number of races in which there is reliable previous form, but on the other hand it does prevent you falling into a very well-known trap. How often do you hear punters or journalists, who should know better, talk about 'luck' - and that magic phrase 'if only', as in : 'He would have won last time out, if only he hadn't been crowded at the first'. In many races, there are several 'if only' dogs, and you can rack your brain for hours trying to assess their chances.

The number of 'reliable' races varies from track to track. From my records of the higher graded races (A1-A3), it is about 30% of all such races at the average track. The proportion is probably lower in the lower grades, A4-A8. At some tracks, such as Walthamstow, which has long straights, but rather tight bends, the proportion is considerably lower. The best distance and track is the 523 metres at Hackney. The long (120 m) run to the first bend ensures that the dogs sort themselves out before the first bend. I find that over 60% of the races here provide a reliable result.

Now you have a series of time figures from each race, and, if you agree with my remarks above, a reliable series from about 30% of all races. How do you use these figures to find winners?

The obvious answer would be to compile the figures for all the dogs in a race, and to select the dog with the highest time figure. For once, the obvious would be the wrong thing to do, for two reasons. It would overlook the relation between time and grade; and fail to consider the way the race was run.

TIME FOR THE GRADE

Consider the following table of times (using the index) for an 'M3' grade at Hackney.

Trap 1 Arthur 78

Trap 2 Billy   63

Trap 3 Camilla Trial time

Trap 4 Dave   Trial time

Trap 5 Eddie   83

Trap 6 Fred   85

TRIAL TIMES

You will note that I have not recorded the times of Traps 3 and 4, which previously ran in a trial. Even if these were 4 dog trials, the experience of running against 3 other dogs is not the same as running against 5, so I always discount trial times.

Dogs are often made favourite on the strength of a good trial time - I would never back such a dog, as a trial is quite unlike the real thing. Even if the time was faster than that of any of those recorded in a race, I would still back the dog with a good race time to win.

Although you should never follow trial times into a race, you should always check through trial times for future reference. A dog which shows a steady improvement in trial times, and, more significantly, in sectional times, should be noted for the future. Trials often give significant clues to the way in which a dog is likely to run (ie railer, wide runner), but trial times should not be taken in isolation.

Assume for the sake of example, that all these times were from reliable races, recorded last time out, and in the same grade. In practice, this rarely happens, and we may have to go back a few races to find a reliable figure.

In this example, Fred seems to be the obvious selection. But although he has the fastest time of the dogs here, he has not achieved a good time for the grade. This is where a knowledge of the time for the grade comes in. For an M3 the average time is 100, with the minimum time 90.

I calculate the minimum for each grade by taking 10 points from the average time, so that the tables look as follows :

M3 90-100

M2 110-120

M1 115-125

The first figure is the minimum qualifying figure for the grade; the second is the average figure for the grade.

The principle is the same whatever the distance - thus for 484 metre races ('A'), in which the average times for the grades are slightly differently distributed, the index figures are as follows :

A3 90-100

A2 95-105

A1 110-120

Again, the first figure is the minimum qualifying figure for the grade; the second is the average figure.

Our table of figures for this race immediately tells us that we are dealing with a race which is of poor quality for this grade. This shows one of the great advantages of time as an indicator. In horse racing, some quite ordinary fields turn out for high-class handicaps (say 0-110), yet it takes some experience and checking through the form of each horse to be able to assess the overall quality of the field. Using a time index, this is immediately obvious.

Secondly, as none of the dogs with reliable race times has yet shown anything quite of M3 class, s/he may well be outrun by a dog with only trial times. I usually find that these races are uncompetitive and that it would be unwise to back the fastest time dog.

In the example used above, all the dogs had run in the same grade. If we had a dog with a 90+ time, then we would be interested - this is the simplest case. Much more frequently, we have dogs which have been running in different grades. How do we interpret time and grade here?

A dog which is upgraded will often record a markedly slower time, even if he has not been hampered. As a rule, he will find the faster early pace of higher grade races too much to cope with, and fade badly in the later stages of the race. Thus a dog capable of 100 in an M3 grade, may only be able to record 80 in an M2. In this case, the correct figure to look for is his time figure for this grade time, not his most recent figure in a higher grade.

The most difficult case of all is the 'grade jumper'. Say if a dog records 109 in an M3 grade. This is a very good time for the grade, being 9 points above average, and the grader will have to take drastic steps. What is the chance of this dog if then put into an M2 grade?

Here we have to distinguish between the dog which is going into an M2 grade for the first time, and the dog which has in the past won an M2. In the first case, you should not bet. If, however, the dog won an M2 some time ago with a time of 110+, and his recent time figures are on the rise, then clearly he is coming back to his best form and has a good chance of jumping the grade. This is yet another example of how important it is to keep thorough, well-indexed records over a period of time.

RACING STYLE

So far we have got some idea of the times various dogs can achieve in this grade. This is no more than simple arithmetic - now we come to the difficult part : racing style.

Most dogs have a racing style which is fairly consistent throughout their career. Two types should be noted, which can be dismissed from our calculations as far as finding winners is concerned, but which must never be left out of our overall assessment: the chasers and the faders.

'Chasers' will run on gamely behind the leading dogs, but in a cleanly run race will rarely find enough speed to pass those in front to win. They may run on in a fast time, to be a close up second and third, but it would be unwise to rely on this time in the future. They will win races every now and then if left clear by a melee in front, when they may have enough pace to run on to win. These are genuine dogs - but not unlucky.

Sometimes such a dog will attract press comment on the lines of : 'his turn is near', 'deserves reward for his consistency' : on the strength of which he will be made favourite. If you are convinced he is a 'chaser' you should follow your own judgement, and resist the temptation to back him. The press comment can be good news for us if as a result our selection is pushed out in price.

'Faders' may run very fast to the first or second bend, but then live up to their name. These dogs are difficult to win with, as they are always vulnerable to a strong galloping dog overtaking them. They can win if there is a melee behind them, leaving them clear to run on and win. If this happens, however, their overall time will be fairly slow for the grade, and you won't be misled into supporting them next time out. These dogs can cause a problem for your selection, by running fast to the first bend, causing the other dogs to crowd.

The two main types of winning style we should look for are : the early paced type; and the late finisher. These are the most easily recognisable types - some dogs do run in either way in different races, but it is rare to find this ability among graded racers, though it is not uncommon in Open Race competitors.

Not all winning types fit into these clear-cut categories. The most difficult type to categorise is the one which runs at an average pace to the first bend, but emerges from the second bend in the lead, or in the back straight, galloping on relentlessly to win. It is very difficult to weigh up such a dog's chances, because it's hard to predict whether he will be able to take the lead at the second bend. Although such a dog cannot be left out of our calculations, I am quite wary of betting on this type of dog.

Of the early paced dogs, the dog which sticks close to the rails (the 'railer') running from trap 1 or 2 is perhaps a better bet, than the wide dog in trap 5 or 6, or even the dog which runs towards the middle of the track. Obviously the railer covers much less ground than the other types, greatly to his advantage.

My records show that fast-starting dogs from Trap 6 have a poor record. It may be that such dogs run wider from the outside trap than they do from Trap 5. This tendency seems to be more pronounced at Wembley which does not have banked bends.

The only way to get a good knowledge of a dog's racing style is to go and see for yourself - seemingly obvious advice, but next time you are at the track, see how many of the spectators are watching closely and making notes. Concentrate on what happens at the first bend - this is where a dog's running style will have the most impact on his running in this and future races. A good place to stand at the track is at the end of the run-up to the first bend, from where you can see whether a dog starting from an inside trap is a true railer or runs in his own lane; similarly whether a wide runner from an outside trap runs straight but wide (because he is running from a wide trap) or actually moves to his right.

The second most important point in the race is when the runners come off the final bend. At this point a true railer will continue to run close to the rails, whereas a dog which has railed earlier in the race but is not a true railer will move to the middle. A true strong finisher will run dead straight to the line, while the tired dogs tend to move wide from this point.

The position on the finishing post which seems to be the favourite for most punters is actually the least important. There is not a great deal to learn by looking at the finish - in any case the press reports normally give full details. If you look at the video recording after you have watched the race from the head-on position, you will have as full an outlook on the race as possible.

To return to the early paced dogs : if a dog wins in this style, how can we be confident that he will do so next time out? After all, he could have been a fast starter in a field of slow finishers. Here we have to rely on the sectional times, the information we really need being the time to the first bend. Unfortunately this is not recorded on any English, Irish or Scottish track, so unless you can record this time yourself at the track, you have to make do with the time to the winning post first time round.

There is another shortcoming with the sectional times provided in the press. Unlike the time for the whole race, there is no allowance for going calculated for the the sectional times. I suggest that in races around 475 metres, you divide the going allowance by 8 to give an allowance for the sectional time; and around 520 metres, divide by 5. This is because in the former case, the distance to the point at which the sectional time is calculated is around 1/8th of the distance of the race, in the latter case around 1/5th.

Thus if the sectional for a 523 metre race at Hackney is given as 5.95, with a going allowance of +.20, then add .04 to the sectional - the adjusted sectional is 5.99. An adjustment of 4/100ths of a second may seem to be over-precise, but consider the following example.

On different race days, with an overall going allowance of +20 on one and -20 on the other, two dogs record sectionals of 6.00. In the former case, the adjusted sectional is 6.04; and in the latter 5.96. That is, the difference between the two is 8/100 ths of a second, equivalent to one length - quite a crucial difference at this stage of the race.

To be safe, I consider that an early paced dog must have at least .05 second in hand over his rivals to avoid being crowded at the first bend. This is just over half a length, or about half a metre.

Here are my rules for using sectional times as a guide to the chances of early paced dogs running from different traps :

TRAP 1 : 0.05 seconds in hand over Trap 2

TRAP 2 : 0.05 seconds in hand over Traps 1 and 3

TRAP 3 : 0.05 seconds in hand over all the other Traps

TRAP 4 : 0.10 seconds in hand over all the other Traps

TRAP 5 : 0.05 seconds in hand over Traps 4 and 6

TRAP 6 : 0.05 seconds in hand over Trap 6

The time for Trap 6 is purely notional, because as I have said above, fast starters have a poor record from this trap. The most difficult traps are traps 3 and 4, especially for 'railers', which have to cut across the dogs in the inside traps to get to the front.

Not only must an early paced dog have a relative advantage over the other dogs, he must also be able to run up to or beat the sectional time for the grade. For example, the average sectional time for A2 races at Hackney is 3.89 seconds . To guard against any surprises in what *seems* to be a field of slow starters, your selection must be able to run to 3.89 or better.

With this type of dog, it is also advisable to look at his sectional times over the last few races. If these show a steady improvement, this is an additional sign that the dog is in good form. This applies particularly to bitches, especially after their seasonal rest, when they can make phenomenal improvement not only on their overall time, but also on their sectional times.

As I have pointed out above, the sectional times available on British and Irish tracks are times to the winning post first time round. Therefore, they are only of any use at the shorter distances. This distance varies with different tracks - clearly the longer the run to this point, the more informative the sectional time.

In a 640m or 660m race, the dogs have already run round two bends before they reach the winning post first time round, so the sectional time to this point is not very informative. However, at some tracks (for example, Wimbledon) this is counterbalanced by the long run to the first bend, which means that there is little crowding or baulking at that point.

I must say that I favour the other type of dog - the strong late finisher. There is more chance of a reliably improving early paced dog being beaten to the first bend, or crowded there, than there is of a fast finisher either failing to deliver a late challenge or of being baulked while doing so. **A slow-starting late finisher is a particularly good bet in a field of fast starters** - the latter will in all probability bunch at the first or second bend or have run each other ragged by the third or fourth bend.

The real danger here is that your selection may be crowded by other slow starting dogs at the first bend. Here, too, the sectional times are a useful guide - to be on the safe side, your selection should be at least .05 seconds *slower* than his rivals. Essentially the same figures apply as above, with the values reversed.

TRAP 1 : 0.05 seconds behind Trap 2

TRAP 2 : 0.05 seconds behind Traps 1 and 3

TRAP 3 : 0.05 seconds behind all the other Traps

TRAP 4 : 0.10 seconds behind all the other Traps

TRAP 5 : 0 .05 seconds behind Traps 4 and 6

TRAP 6 : 0.05 seconds behind Trap 6

A dog with this running style obviously has a much better chance in the outside traps. From the inside traps, there may be other dogs blocking the run in. **A dog which runs wide, but has enough pace to come with a late run to win, is one of the safest bets in racing.**

Using your form record as a basis, you should now compile an index card for each dog. As soon as you begin to tabulate all this information, a clear picture of a dog's ability, running style, and recent form will begin to emerge. If you keep a simple record card of every race run by each dog, this information will be easy to analyse.

Even better, store this information on a computer - the 'search' command will enable you to check various aspects of performance very quickly and (providing the information has been entered in the correct form in the first place!) without error.

For example, look at the record of WEEKLY EXPRESS, running at Hackney over 523 metres in April and May 1988.

WEEKLY EXPRESS b d July 1985 Duggan

Race	Time	Position	Grade	Trap	Style	Sectional
04	61	(4)	M3	T2	r.o.	6.24
05	83	(1)	M3	T3	s.a., fin well	6.27
08	(77)	(4)	M3	T4	r.o.	6.25
13	(NR)	(6)	M3	T3	cwd 1	6.16
22	(105)	(4)	M3	T3	ev. ch.	6.14

(finds it difficult to win in M3)

Race	Time	Position	Grade	Trap	Style	Sectional
24	NR	(4)	M3	T3	blkd 1	6.17
26	61	(3)	M3	T3	s.a., r.o.	6.19
28	71	(3)	M3	T3	ev. ch.	6.17
30	64	(2)	M3	T3	s.a., r.o.	6.16
38	66	(5)	M3	T3	s.a., blkd 1	6.27

Note : the underlined times are from reliable races.

At a glance, you can see that the running style of WEEKLY EXPRESS is to get away slowly with a sectional of around 6.20., and run on usually avoiding trouble, but without quite enough speed to win, except in Race 05. In his last 5 races, he has 3 reliable times of 61, 64, 66, so that you could reasonably assume that he would run to a time of around 65. Therefore, in his current form, and in this grade, you could quite confidently discount his chances.

When you have two or three reliable figures from recent races, you can allocate a time - for - grade figure. This is quite a simple case : if you gave WEEKLY EXPRESS a figure of 65 for M3, you should not be too far out.

Of course, it isn't always as simple as this - but the main point to remember is that you should concentrate on the reliable figures (underlined in the above example).

After you have recorded about 5 races, you should write down your opinion of the dog's ability *immediately* after its latest race. Next time the dog appears, it will be invaluable to have your opinion recorded when it was fresh in your mind.

Try to anticipate under what conditions he can win - for example, if you write 'Can win a weak M3 from Trap 2', you are **anticipating** what conditions the dog needs rather than **reacting** to the racecard when it appears.

How far back should you go for these figures? I only rely on the figures shown in the last month. Your long-term records will be invaluable, as they will tell you under what conditions (grade/trap) a dog gave his best performance. This is especially useful if a dog is raised in grade - you will then know whether he has won in this higher grade before, and, if so, from which trap.

This may seem quite a lot of work, but if you compile your records regularly and do not allow a backlog to build up, then it will take no more than ten minutes per race to write up your form book and the associated records for each dog. If you confine yourself to the top grade dogs, say A1-A3, then you will have records on between 50-100 dogs, depending on the track.

Once you have the information readily available in this form, it is a matter of moments to weigh up the chances of most of the runners. In the average graded race, there will be 3 or even 4 dogs who are there really to make up the numbers, and you can focus on the chances of 2 or 3 which, on their time performance and running style, seem to be in with a chance.

Here is an example of a pre-race analysis, an M3 (523 metres) run at Hackney on 14 June 1988.

Trap 1 FIRE STICK 100 M3 probably out of form

Trap 2 CLIPPER SHIP 90 M3 reasonable recent form

Trap 3 RAY'S MAGPIE 105 M3 523m too far

Trap 4 HIGHFIELD BUSH 111 M3 T4 finds M2 too difficult, in good form

Trap 5 THREE SPEED 98* M3 can win by staying on

Trap 6 APRIL FOX 108* M3 fortunate to win

Note : the underlined figures denote reliable time; the asterisk indicates a winner in this grade during the last month.

Purely on time for the grade, HIGHFIELD BUSH appears to have a good chance - at 4-1, she was certainly a good value bet.

This method of analysis will not always point so such a clear-cut selection, but what it will do is show whether this is a competitive race for the grade. For example, a race may be entirely made up of dogs which have not win in this grade - this is a race to avoid. Or it may include dogs which have won in this grade, but in a slow time, showing that this is a weak race.

One of the great advantages of greyhound racing is that the cards appear in the sporting press the day before racing. Unlike horse racing, you don't have to wait for the overnight declaration stage.

Very occasionally (less than a dozen occasions a month at, say, Hackney), on the day of the race a dog may be withdrawn if off-colour, or a bitch if she has come into season. The reserves are usually not of the highest standard for the grade, so there is little danger of a very good dog being put in at the last moment. If you are not at the track, this information is usually available on the bookmakers' screens for BAGS races.

There are only 6 runners to analyse so if you have methodically indexed the information for every dog to appear so far, then you should be able to collate the time for the grade figures in a matter of minutes.

Time for the grade is the basis of selection, but other factors do have to be taken into account. Before you make your final selection, you need to consider a number of other factors, analysed in the next chapter.

CHAPTER 4

Winning Factors

Say that you have selected a dog which has the best time in the race, a winning time for the grade, and whose running style should ensure that he or she gets a clear run. You still have to consider the following factors, listed in order of importance : recent form; fitness; age; sex; going; time of the year; number of runners; distance; and weight.

RECENT FORM

The only good form in greyhound racing is recent form. In horse racing, you could confidently back a horse which has won and then reappeared some 6 or 8 weeks later, whereas it would be very unwise to do so with a greyhound.

Greyhounds run far more often than racehorses, and their form goes in cycles. They always run consistently, but *at a certain level*. When they run into form, they will be capable of winning two or three races within, say, a 30 day period.

If you record each dog's performance carefully, as I have suggested, you will see when a dog is running into form. A very useful indicator is the sectional time - if this shows gradual improvement, then the dog is running into form. **However, don't anticipate too much - it is advisable to wait to see the dog win a race as indisputable proof that he is on the winning trail.**

Conversely, you will see when a dog has gone 'off the boil' - he will run consistently, perhaps setting up a series of closely placed seconds and thirds, but will have temporarily lost that vital edge essential to winning. This is when to beware of those fatal phrases so beloved by journalists - 'overdue for a win', 'his turn is near', 'deserves consolation.'

FITNESS

Greyhounds' level of fitness seems to vary more than that of racehorses - both their form and their fitness seem to go in cycles. A fit dog walks out onto the track alert, looking round him intently, his head up and ears cocked, and his tail high and waving; an unfit dog walks listlessly, often with his head hardly moving - now you know the meaning of the expressions 'tail between his legs' and 'hangdog look'!

The difference between fitness and unfitness is less marked in bitches. Even at their fittest, they don't seem to show as much interest in their surroundings as their male counterparts. However, the tell-tale signs are the same, even if less prominent.

You should never back a dog just because he is the fittest looking in the field - but it is absolutely essential that your form choice looks fit and raring to go. You cannot really see this by watching the race on the SIS - you have to be there at the track to judge a dog's fitness.

AGE

Dogs are allowed to run in a trial at the age of 15 months. Till they are 2 years old, they are officially 'puppies'. Most of their physical development takes place during this period, and the better class puppies climb rapidly up the grades to reach Open Race standard, frequently by the time they reach their second birthday.

Being much less physically developed than their elders, puppies are likely to lose out in a barging match. Puppies are often inconsistent at the traps, sometimes leaving the traps slowly or stumbling at the start. Unless you know that a puppy is well built and of a good weight compared to his rivals, you are certainly taking a chance backing a puppy against older dogs.

I find that the best age range is from 2 years to 3 years 6 months, for both dogs and bitches. Greyhounds reach their full physical and racing maturity during this period, and a clear racing style, trap preference, level of ability has emerged about half way through this period.

During this period, a good grader will move up and down the grades between A3 to A1, but after about 2y 3m is unlikely to rise any higher than this. Every so often a dog will run into form and win 2 or 3 races in a row. This is what you must be prepared to take advantage of - but don't anticipate too much : wait till he has actually won a race before considering a selection.

This is where keeping good records is absolutely vital. For example, a dog may win in a good time for an A2 race, but not quite good enough for an A1. If he is upgraded, you should not back him, but should wait until the grader puts him back into an A2. Provided that he is not put into too difficult a trap (and your records will indicate whether this is so), he is a very good bet to win again. **However, dogs only seem to retain their form for 30 days, and if he returns to his grade only after this period has elapsed, then you should not bet.**

After 3 years 6 months, dogs begin to lose their edge slightly - particularly those which rely on early speed for victory. You should look very carefully at the chance of any dog over 3 years 6 months which has this running style. With the late-finishing type, I do not back dogs or bitches older than 4 years. When they are older than that, they may still win the occasional race, but cannot be relied on to win two races in succession.

SEX

Bitches are much more lightly built than dogs, usually weighing in around 25kg, as compared to 32 kg for the average dog. This means that they are more handy, being able to run closer to the rails and go through narrower gaps. On the debit side, they are likely to suffer more if they collide with dogs.

Once or twice a year a bitch may come into season, after which : 'A bitch may not run in any Trial or Race...for a minimum period of ten weeks nor until, in the opinion of the Racecourse Veterinary Surgeon, it is fit to do subsequently.' (Rule 56). The season can now be suppressed (noted in the racecard as 'Ssn suppressed'), though this is not very common. Also a bitch may not come into season for the first time until relatively late in life.

Just before coming into season, a bitch will often given greatly improved performances, excelling anything she has achieved previously. On her return from season, a bitch will run well below her previous form, but may then show a rapid return to form. This usually happens in the period 16-20 weeks after the seasonal date.

Keep good records of bitches performance in relation to their seasonal date (if known, it is given in the racecard). Once she begins to show sign of returning to form by winning a race (*not* a trial), pay very close attention to her progress. A particularly encouraging sign is a steady decrease in sectional times. Bitches which win by early pace can often show a very marked increase in initial acceleration.

In my experience, once a bitch does start to improve under these

circumstances, the usual strict requirements of time performance for the grade can be waived. The only proviso is that the bitch should have recorded the fastest time of all the competitors last time out, and that this time should be above 50 on an index figure. You then have a very good bet indeed - probably the best in the entire range of greyhound racing, often at a good price, as other backers often seem to ignore this opportunity.

But don't anticipate such improvement - a bitch may *appear* to be coming into form, running well close up in second and third place. It is advisable to wait until a bitch has really confirmed she is coming back to her best by winning. Sometimes it does happen that a bitch returning from season puts up a number of promising performances, but does not win during this period. Oddly enough, bitches which run in this way often attract more favourable press coverage (of the kind 'her turn is near after her return from season') than those which have actually won. Indeed, punters seem to be *more* sceptical in the latter case, and such winners are often at rewarding odds next time out.

Even outside the period after returning from seasonal rest, bitches are very reliable. Once they run into form and win a race, they can be confidently backed to win again - even if they are raised a grade. In fact, the only time I feel in any way confident about backing a 'grade jumper' is when a bitch is involved.

Bitches also possess exceptional stamina - a bitch with winning form in a race of 640 metres and over is a very good bet, because she is certain to stay the trip in a fast run race, whereas dogs do not as a rule have the same degree of stamina.

Because of their size and build, bitches are very 'handy' runners. When they are in form their manoeuvrability gives them considerable advantages when running round tight circuits (such as Catford or Romford) or where there is usually a considerable amount of scrimmaging (Walthamstow).

GOING

Within certain limits, changes in the going do not appear to have much effect on racing performance. When the going does get soft (indicated by a going allowance of -50 or more), I do not take into account form shown under such conditions. Likewise, if it is possible to anticipate that the going will be so soft, or if you are at the track and can see that it is, then it is wisest not to bet. Form tends to be unreliable, and the softer the going, the more approximate the going allowances become.

If you are at the track in these circumstances, and must bet, then watch the first three or four races closely. The going may get much softer on the inside of the circuit, giving the outside traps a considerable advantage.

TIME OF THE YEAR

The open racers do have a season, which roughly follows that of the Flat racing season, with the Derby at the end of June and the Cesarewitch at the end of September.

But there is no season as far as graded racing is concerned. Unlike Flat racing, where early season form (ie in the first two months) can be quite unreliable because many of the contestants are not fit, graded racers are ready to go at any time of the year.

The only limiting factor here is the state of the going. Throughout the summer, going variations on grass or sand tracks are fairly minimal (say from +30 to -20 on sand) and can be ignored when assessing form. Even in a wet summer, which makes life very difficult for followers of Flat racing, sand tracks drain quickly enough not to pose any problems.

However, certain times of the year are very much more favourable than others for following form.

February-March. These are usually the wettest months of the year, and the variability of the going frequently causes shock results. The variations are more marked at the grass tracks (Hove and Walthamstow), but even on sand the going can change from day to day. Some sand tracks are relaid during this period, and until the sand has settled down the track runs slow.

Even in a dry winter, when there are few racing days with the going slower than -50 (when I have suggested that you should not bet - see above, GOING), the standard of graded racing seems at its lowest during these months. This may be because racing in general is less competitive - there are very few important Open Races on the flat.

It is is a good idea not to bet at all during this period - in fact, if you take a complete break from racing during this period it won't do you any harm at all. You will begin the season in the Spring mentally refreshed and ready to concentrate on the most important period for the backer.

April-June. The Open Race season begins in earnest with the Blue Riband (490m) at Wembley, and culminating in the Derby at the end of June. Stimulated by the competition from the higher class dogs, the graded runners seem to be of much better quality during this period. Perhaps the season has something to do with it - in the bracing atmosphere of spring and early summer, the good dogs seem to be alert, on their toes, and ready to do their best. The puppies which have been learning to race in the previous autumn are now strong, fit 2 year olds.

This is the period the wise backer should concentrate on as this is the most reliable period in the year for greyhound form. It is the equivalent in horse racing terms to the period from the end of the Royal Ascot meeting (end of June) to the Ayr Western Meeting (mid-September). This is the period I have selected for analysis in the next chapter.

Runners which record a good time can often show good form again in the Autumn - this is where good record-keeping will pay dividends.

July-mid September. The period after the Derby meeting seems something of an anti-climax. Although there are numerous good quality Open Races, form does not work out very well during these middle and end of the summer (July, August, and roughly the first half of September). The dogs which showed good form in the spring and early summer seem to need a mid-season break; and they also lack the stimulus of competition from the puppies, whose season does not begin until the autumn.

It is best to bet very sparingly, if at all, during this period. I usually restrict myself to the safest bet - the bitch returning from her seasonal rest. You should, however, keep up your time records - this will prove invaluable when you come to the next period.

Mid September - January. In most recent years the autumn has been dry and there have been relatively minor variations in going. This is the part of the season when the puppies generally make their debut - they seem to give a spur to the older dogs.

During this period, you should look out for runners which have recorded a good time in the April-June period, and which are returning after a rest. A dog which is two years old in September or October can find several winning opportunities during this period.

NUMBER OF RUNNERS

6 runner races offer the best opportunities, as in 8 runner races there is much more likelihood of interference. Occasionally, 1 or even 2 dogs may be withdrawn from a race, leaving a field of 5 or 4. Your selection has a correspondingly greater chance, as there is much less chance of baulking or bumping.

However, it does not pay to follow the form of these races, as it is not a realistic guide to a race in which there is a full complement of runners.

DISTANCE

This does not usually pose many problems - by the time a dog is 2y 3m you should have a fairly good idea of the distance he prefers.

Some experts advocate watching dogs closely after the finishing post, to see whether they run on strongly, as a guide to their probable performance over a longer distance.

This theory has always seemed rather ill-founded, if only because at most tracks the differences between the distances are so substantial that you can't really draw any sensible conclusions from performance at the shorter distance. For instance, at Walthamstow, the 'S' distance is 165 metres or 34% further than the 'A' distance. The only plausible case is Hackney, where 'M' races are 38 metres (8%) longer than 'A' races. Even here, it is advisable to consider form only from the same distance.

WEIGHT

Some backers try to make a system of watching a dog's racing weight very closely, noting the weight recorded when a dog wins for future reference. Obviously, this has something to be said for it, but it can only be one of a number of factors, and a very minor one at that. I must say that I rarely find changes in racing weight to be a particularly significant indicator.

CHAPTER FIVE
A Typical Season

To show how my approach works in practice, I will now look at results obtained in a sample period of a typical season, 1988.

You can apply my methods to look for the winner of every graded race or Open race run in heats at any time of the season, and if you did I am sure you would make a profit. But in my book it pays to be selective, so that you can make as much, if not more profit, while spending far less time.

I concentrate on the following tracks and grades: Hackney ('A' and 'M'); Hove ('A'); Walthamstow ('A'); Wembley ('A'); and Wimbledon ('S'). At Hackney, Hove and Wimbledon I back runners of any style provided they are in a suitable trap; whereas at Walthamstow and Wembley, I am more selective (see Chapter Seven which gives detailed information on these and other tracks). As you will see from the remainder of the chapter, you can find enough opportunities in the best part of the season (ie from April to the end of June) to make a handsome profit.

All the information you need is readily available in the racing press, and it is a simple matter to keep your own list of dogs which win in good time and style. You should go racing as often as you can, but strictly speaking it is only necessary to go when you intend to place a bet. What is so often claimed for horse racing systems - 'Make your selection in a few minutes reading of the daily press' - is really true here.

In addition to the daily press, you will find the weekly page of reports on greyhound racing in the *Raceform Handicap Book* absolutely invaluable. It is the equivalent to the *Raceform Notebook* and gives full reports of graded racers which have run well. No other daily or weekly paper does this, and its reports are indispensable for finding winners.

What you do need is patience. Even in the best part of the season, there may be a week or more without any opportunities - and then there may be two on one day, as can be seen from the records below.

In this chapter , I analyse the races in which I considered having a bet; in the next chapter, I explain my *betting strategy* which will help you maximise profits.

19 APRIL: WIMBLEDON S2. As it happened I began with a safe bet - a bitch returning from season. MISS MENDER had won an S3 a week ago in a slow time for the grade of 76, but this was still a faster time than any other dog had recorded last time out over this distance. She was 131 days out of her season, her sectional time had shown improvement so, as this was a weak field for an S2 , I thought she had a worthwhile chance. Winning at 9-2 she gave me a good start to the season.

26 APRIL: WALTHAMSTOW A3. A3. This race shows the importance of time for the grade. GRACIOUS FRIEND had won an A3 with a late finish from Trap 4 two weeks ago, with a time of 100, ie a qualifying time for the grade. He was opposed by AND THAT'S THAT (Trap 2) with a time of 102 for A4 and HANOVER DANDY (Trap 5), also a winner of an A4, in 101: but GRACIOUS FRIEND was now in the best trap at the track, and looked a very good bet. He won with a late finish, at 100-30 neither had won an A3.

30 APRIL: WIMBLEDON S1. I thought I had another good bet in WEIGH

IN GAL. Running from Trap 4, she had won her previous race, also an S1, from the same trap in the good time of 158. She looked well enough, and there did not seem to be any other dog in the race with comparable form. However, in the race itself she did not show her customary early speed , was soon headed and had no chance thereafter, coming home a loser at 8-1. The winner, MURLEN'S SAIL, galloped on strongly in the final straight to win in the good time of 169 and went into my notebook.

4 MAY: WEMBLEY A6. This is at a lower grade than I would consider if a dog was involved, but on the other hand an A6 at Wembley is often of higher quality than the nominally equivalent grade at other tracks. ROSEHIP JOY (2y 3m), who was 123 days out of her season, had won an A7 from Trap 4., in the best style for Wembley - running on well at the finish. Her time of 77 last time out was faster than that of any other competitor. At 9-4 she started at a shorter price than I had expected from the newspaper forecasts, but was still a good bet.

My first selection ran exactly as she had done in her previous race, coming with a late flourish in the home straight to win well.

5 MAY : WIMBLEDON S1. MURLEN'S SAIL, which I had noted on 30 April when beating my selection WEIGH IN GAL, ran against three dogs he had beaten in his previous race - WEIGH IN GAL, GO ROVING, KILLURE OPINION. All these three seemed rather out of form, and although MURLEN'S SAIL now ran from Trap 3 (in his earlier race he had been in Trap 1), I do not consider this a difficult trap at Wimbledon. He looked fit and well, and justified my confidence by winning at 6-1.

7 MAY: HOVE OPEN RACE. The Open race season was beginning to warm up, and I very much liked BAD INTENTIONS in the Phoenix Brewery Greyhound Olympic 1st Semi-Final. In his previous race, he had recorded a very fast sectional of 4.39 and overall time of 154. Previously in trap 3, he was now better drawn in Trap 2. None of the runners seemed to have comparable form, and in the circumstances 9-4 seemed to be quite a generous price. Once again, he showed blistering early speed to win well.

17 MAY: WIMBLEDON S3. This race showed the value of keeping your own records. LOST GIRL (3y 2m), 125 days out of her season, had won an S4 on 7 May from Trap 4, yet this form line was omitted from the Sporting Life card. She was the fastest runner on her time in her previous race (78).

This was a weak field for an S3, and running from Trap 3, LOST GIRL had a clear chance. Perhaps because of the newspaper's mistake, my selection was overlooked by the tipsters, and as it turned out, by the punters as well. Unless I had had my own records to refer to, I would have been in the same position - as it was, 5-1 against'the selection was a gift. Quickly away, she was never headed, and came home in a faster time (88).

19 MAY: WIMBLEDON : S2 LOST GIRL was out again fairly quickly. This time she faced a more serious competitor, QUAINTON DOLLY in Trap 2, who had won an S3 last time out from the same trap, with an improving sectional. However, her time was 1 spot slower, and I decided that LOST GIRL was still improving enough to win in this higher grade.

An indication of the sentimental approach many punters have was that the short-priced favourite was ARUMAD in Trap 3. In his last two races, both in this grade, he had recorded times of 74 and 70, running very much in the style of a chaser. Yet the newspaper tipsters made him their first selection - listening to the punters in the betting ring, I heard the familiar refrains 'his turn is near' 'deserves to win soon.'

Neither LOST GIRL nor QUAINTON DOLLY was strongly fancied, and I took 9-2 about the former. Unfortunately, she trailed in a well-beaten last, showing that her run of success was now over - QUAINTON DOLLY won by one length, but in a slow time for this grade of 84.

26 MAY : HACKNEY M2. This seemed a fairly clear-cut race. Last time out, ON MY OWN had won an M2 in 131, beating BRINDLE MAN by 1^1/$_4$ lengths. They met on exactly the same terms, running from the same traps (6 and 5 respectively). Both had the same late-finishing style, but there seemed no reason why ON MY OWN should not win again, particularly since BRINDLE MAN was now 3 years 7 months old. They were joint favourites at 2-1 but ON MY OWN ran a poor race, to finish 11/4 lengths behind BRINDLE MAN, who won in 108.

31 MAY : HACKNEY A3. Just over two weeks earlier, I had noted RIVER ROAD HERO winning a well-contested A3 with a strong late finish, in 103. He had since run in an A2, M2 and M2, without making much impression. Back to a suitable grade, he was opposed by THREE SPEED, who won an A3 in 104, but this was an unreliable race. Furthermore THREE SPEED was now 3 years and 1 month - perhaps over the top for his running style. As if to show how consistent dogs can be, RIVER ROAD HERO won in 102, at the useful price of 9-2.

2 JUNE : HACKNEY M3 HIGHFIELD BUSH (2y 3m) starting from Trap 4 had won her previous race, also from Trap 4, in a reliable time of 85. Her sectional time of 5.98 was a good one for this grade, and also a notable improvement over that of her previous race over this distance (2 April) of 6.13 (calculated).

I thought that there were two main dangers. On his last race in this grade, CARLING FORD BOY had recorded a reliable 94, with a respectable sectional of 6.02 (calculated). SPORTING BEAUTY (1y 11m), also a bitch, had won an M4, a reliable race, in 94, with a sectional of 6.05, from Trap 4.

However, HIGHFIELD BUSH's win last time out in the same grade and trap seemed too good to ignore. Further, SPORTING BEAUTY was running in a higher grade and from a different trap (now Trap 6). Although her sectional last time out was an improvement on earlier performances, she was still a puppy and would not be able to cope with HIGHFIELD BUSH's early pace.

As it turned out, CARLING FORD BOY did not run, simplifying matters somewhat. In the circumstances, 7-2 seemed a fair price which I was happy to accept. HIGHFIELD BUSH showed virtually the same early speed (sectional of 5.99) to beat SPORTING BEAUTY by 2 3/4 lengths in a good time of 111.

14 JUNE : HACKNEY M3 The next race was much simpler to weigh up. HIGHFIELD BUSH had run in an M2 on 9 June against much faster dogs. Starting from Trap 3, she was bumped on the run in and finished a well beaten last. Here she was back in her preferred trap and grade, with no real dangers.

For some reason, there was a very open market in this race, with 4 dogs at 4-1, the others at 9-2 and 5-1. Given that my selection seemed to have an outstanding chance, 4-1 was a price which could not be missed!

She won in an almost identical to that of 2 June, recording a sectional of 5.97 and an overall figure of 116.

16 JUNE: WIMBLEDON S1 In this race, WEIGH IN GAL (2y 9m) had an obvious chance. Last time out, she was well beaten in an Open Race over 820 metres, but on 31 May she had won an S1 from the same trap (4) in a reasonable time of 127.

No other runner had shown winning form of this calibre : the only recent winner in the grade was STORM HOUSE, a winner on 4 June in a slow time of 87.

Here the price (5-4) was a pretty accurate reflection of the form, and so it proved. WEIGH IN GAL won easily, in a good time of 133.

17 JUNE : WEMBLEY A6 LANDES ROCKET (2y 3m) had won an A7 last time out in 59, and was now in the key period - 119 days after the beginning of her seasonal rest. Her time in the previous race was faster than that of any other competitor, and her sectionals had improved. Finally, she had won in the best style and trap for Wembley - a late finisher running from an outside trap (5).

The newspaper tipsters and the betting favoured NEVER WHISTLE, a 2y 1m old dog, which had run without success in A6 races recently. This was all to the good, as I was able to get 5-1 at the track. Closing at 4-1, LANDES ROCKET won in the same style as in her previous races.

25 JUNE : WIMBLEDON OPEN RACE . This race was the final (of the Daily Mirror Challenge) of an Open race run in heats, so that all the runners had recent form at the track.

In an Open Race, trap positions are allocated by draw, although the wide runners are seeded so that they cannot be drawn into inside traps. This resulted in an unusual change of trap position for CHARMING BETTY (2y 6m), from Trap 1 to Trap 6. She had won her last two heats in times of 185 and 212, much faster than any other competitor, and was able to win either by early pace or by a late finish.

As she was 137 days out of her season, I felt confident that she could overcome any problems which might be posed by the draw. This she did at the reasonable price of 3-1, in a time of 179.

25 JUNE: WIMBLEDON S2 This was rather an unusual race, in that it included a previous winner, WEIGH IN GAL, who had been *downgraded* after a victory in S1, into an S2. Nor had any of the other runners recorded faster times - this was obviously a case of the grader being rather short of S2 material at this stage of the season.

WEIGH IN GAL was running from the same trap (4) as last time - again the punters were on the alert, and it was hardly surprising that she was a strong favourite at 6-4. Her winning time of 129 was a slight decrease on her previous performance of 133, but this did not seem to be significant.

SUMMARY OF RESULTS

19 APRIL	Wimbledon	MISS MENDER	W 9-2
26 April	Walthamstow	GRACIOUS FRIEND	W100-30
30 April	Wimbleldon	WEIGH IN GAL	L8-1
4 May	Wembley	ROSEHIP JOY	W9-4
5 May	Wimbledon	MURLEN'S SAIL	W6-1
7 May	Hove	BAD INTENTIONS	W9-4
17 May	Wimbledon	LOST GIRL	W5-1
19 May	Wimbledon	LOST GIRL	L9-2

26 May	Hackney	ON MY OWN	L2-1
31 May	Hackney	RIVER ROAD HERO	W9-2
02 June	Hackney	HIGHFIELD BUSH	W7-2
14 June	Hackney	HIGHFIELD BUSH	W4-1
16 June	Wimbledon	WEIGH IN GAL	W6-4
17 June	Wembley	LANDES ROCKET	W4-1
25 June	Wimbledon	CHARMING BETTY	W3-1
25 June	Wimbledon	WEIGH IN GAL	W5-4

16 selections, 13 winners. 81% winners

CHAPTER SIX

Betting Strategy

Almost every week, it seems, the bookmakers and the Tote compete to devise another method of extracting cash from the punters pockets by offering a new type of bet.

A detailed account of the various types of bets would be out of date soon after this book is published , but the main varieties are roughly similar to those on the Flat. The main exception is the Trio pool on the Tote.

In this type of bet, you have to select 3 dogs, to finish first, second and third in that order. Using the 10p unit, it is quite popular to work out various combinations of 3 dogs to try and win this type of bet.

The wisest course is to avoid all these complicated bets and go for the simple approach - the straightforward win bet with the bookmakers. Let's deal with the latter aspect of this first - why the bookmakers and not the Tote?

Tote betting is very popular at some tracks, more so than betting with the bookmakers. The Tote turnover is very high, and its publicity machine every so often publishes reports of some improbably large sum won for a minuscule stake.

This all sounds very attractive, but in my view there is a fatal drawback to betting on the Tote : you don't know what return you will get, so you can't bet at a price. It is true that the Tote display boards do give approximate odds for each runner, but these can change very quickly. Even if you get on at what seems the very last minute, a final rush of money on one dog can alter the odds very quickly.

Secondly, why go for the straight win bet? Many greyhound punters prefer forecast betting, either straight (naming 2 runners to finish first and second in that order - 1 bet) or reversed (naming 2 runners to finish first and second in either order) forecasts. Reversed forecasts can include 3 dogs - there are then 3 bets.

The rational element in forecast bets lies in the fact that in many greyhound races it is possible to reduce the number of dogs with a real winning chance to two or three. But it doesn't logically follow that a forecast bet involving these dogs is a sound idea. It is quite possible to make a reasonable estimate that one dog will have a clear run, but much harder to do so for two or three dogs.

The main attraction to this type of bet is psychological. Multiple bets involving small stakes give you 'an interest' in every race in which you bet; each loss is quite small; and every so often you will win a gratifyingly large sum for a small stake.

But if you *calculate* what this costs you, you will be very surprised. Say if you have around 20 bets per week (roughly equivalent to betting on half the races at 4 meetings), each multiple bet amounting to £1.00 in all. During the course of a year, you will have staked £1040. The average punter of this type is reckoned to lose 20% of his stake, ie £208. These calculations are based on figures supplied by the bookmakers which probably underestimate the punters' real losses.

Of course this is a small amount (£4.00 per week) to pay for a sociable pastime, and at this rate you are probably betting well within your means. But you'll never make racing pay betting like this; and you'll never improve your strike rate.

So if you want to win at racing, the first rule in betting must be : keep a record of all your bets, even the smallest ones. It is usually the 'fritter' bets which dissipate any substantial winnings you may make.

The second rule is : it is better to wait till everything appears to be in your favour and have a few relatively large bets, than 'take a chance' and have many small multiple bets. In the example given above, it would be better to have 1 bet per week of £20.00, than 20 bets of £1.00.

To do so, refrain from betting or save in some other way until you have a bank of, say, £200, *which you are psychologically prepared to lose* . The size of the bank will vary with individual circumstances - £200 is a fortune to some people, but would be casually thrown away on trivia by others.

This is the golden rule - never bet more than you are prepared to lose, because if you do you will give up too quickly when you lose and you will miss out on the bets which would have set you back on the winning trail.

Now I come to a vital, but very much misunderstood subject - value for money. Every book on betting I've ever read - greyhounds or horses - always states (correctly) that this is the key to successful betting; but none of them states the matter correctly.

The usual argument runs something like this. It attempts to quantify the chances of a given runner, and calculate the corresponding 'correct' odds. Thus :

EVALUATION OF THE RACE	CHANCE	ODDS
1 runner only has an outstanding chance	60%	4 - 6
1 runner only has a very good chance	50%	1 - 1
2 runners have equally good chances	each 33%	2 - 1
3 runners have equally good chances	each 25%	4 - 1

In the first case, if you can get better than 4-6, you are getting value for money. At the odds, you will break even; better than the odds, you will make a profit.

In my opinion, this conception of value for money rests on two fallacies.

Firstly, although the first two cases are quite clear, I think it is only quite rarely that you can say that 2 dogs have *equally* good chances. In other words, I don't think that you can *quantify* chances as precisely as you could if this were a scientific experiment.

It's certainly very misleading to say that 3 runners have *equally* good chances. In a closely graded race, there may well be 3 runners with a chance, but the 'goodness' of these chances is not evenly distributed. This leads to one of the most common misconceptions of value. A punter considers that 3 dogs have a chance, and they are on offer at 7-4, 2-1 and 9-2. *If* these three had *equally* good chances, then 9-2 *would* be the value bet.

Many punters are often not even as clear as this. They may consider that a dog has a 'reasonable' or 'sporting' chance, and when they see it go up at a fairly long price, say 5-1, they will exclaim 'That's the value bet'. In this case, 'value' means nothing more than 'long-priced.' The longer odds often alter a punter's evaluation of a dog's chances.

In looking for value, therefore, you should concentrate on races in which only 1, or, exceptionally, 2 dogs have a very good chance.

Now for the second fallacy concerning value for money. It is that if you can simply 'beat the book' by getting longer odds than the theoretical chance, you will make money in the long run. Thus if there is 1 runner only with a very good chance, you will come out on top if you can get better than 1 - 1 (evens); if 2 runners, better than 2 - 1.

Consider the reality of what you are setting out to do. If you can back a 60% chance at an average price of 5-4 when the real odds are 4-6, ie at twice the real odds, you will make a profit of 35% (in the following discussion, I assume that no tax is paid. For many punters, this is a somewhat unrealistic assumption).

This looks fine in theory, but I think that even a very selective backer will find it hard to select 60% winners over a long period. If you percentage falls to 50%, your rate of return is 12.5%; it only has to fall to 45% for you merely to break even.

The realistic way of looking at value for money, is not to ask, What odds should I accept given a certain strike rate? but What strike rate do I need to maintain in order to make a profit at given odds? The following table will make this clear.

PRICE	STRIKE RATE TO YIELD 50% PROFIT
1 - 1	75%
2 - 1	50%
3 - 1	37%
7 - 2	33%

This is why you should always make your assessment of a race before looking at the odds. Most punters do exactly the opposite - they allow the odds to determine their evaluation of a runner's chances. If they are favourite backers, they will see a runner at 7-4 and say he has a good chance; if they have a mistaken idea of value and see a runner with some chance in at 5-1, they will regard that as the 'value' bet.

Letting the odds determine your view of a dog's chance is - I promise I'll only say this once in this book - letting the tail wag the dog.

If you aim maintain your selections, follow *fixed* principles, then you can take advantage of the *fluctuations* of the odds. To be realistic, you cannot expect to achieve a strike rate of better than 33% - so you should never take odds of less than 7-2. At this price, you can go as low as a 22% strike rate and still come out without loss.

Even if you don't really follow any principle of selection, keep a record of your bets for a few weeks, and work out your profit/loss. Then strike out all those at less than 7-2 and as a rule you will have a much healthier account.

If I can't persuade you to accept such a restriction on your bets, **at least never bet odds on.** Many punters think that professional backers make a living by striking large bets on odds-on chances, sometimes called 'buying money.' Only part of this belief is true - most professional backers have relatively few large bets, rather than a large number of small ones.

But the odds are literally *against* you making a profit by betting in this way. The following table will make this clear :

PRICE   STRIKE RATE TO YIELD 20% PROFIT

4 - 5   66%

4 - 6   72%

4 - 7   77%

1 - 2   80%

You will notice that I have set the profit rate much lower than in the earlier example. You could only make much more than this if you had an extraordinary (I would say impossibly) high strike rate - say 85% at 4 - 5. It would be pointless to accept a much lower percentage return, as you can get 12% from high interest loans on large sums of money,without the risk.

If I still haven't persuaded you *never* to bet odds on, consider the fact that *just to break even* when betting at 4 - 5, you must have a strike rate of 55%. Even in Open Races, in which most of this betting takes place, there are enough upsets to make one avoid this kind of not very highly rewarded risk-taking.

So far I have concentrated on the betting strategy to adopt when you have identified 1 dog with a very good chance. What should you do if you consider that 2 dogs stand clear of their field, and both have an equal chance?

This may seem to be the ideal opportunity for a forecast bet, but for the reasons given above I think this would be a mistake.

If you feel confident that only two dogs in a race have a good chance, it makes more sense to back them both. You can either simply split your normal stake into two halves, or bet according to the odds.

The most common way of doing this is as follows. Say that you think that two dogs have an equal chance, but dog A is at 2-1 and dog B at 4-1. Then vary your stakes so as to win the same amount in each case if a winner : ie put £50 on A (to win £100) and £25 on B (to win £100). If A wins, you win £75; if B wins you win £50. If both lose, you lose £75.00.

It's even worth considering this if you feel that there are two dogs which are clearly better than anything else in the field, although not particularly attractive bets taken in isolation. You could use the top two rated in this way, providing you can get reasonable odds against both - at least 5-2.

This may seem unlikely, but at tracks with strong betting markets, it happens surprisingly often. If you did so, varying your stakes according to the odds, you would get a very good return of 68%.

There is another method of staking which will give you an even higher percentage return (in this case, 86%). Aim to win a given amount (say, £100) on the longer priced selection; and aim to retrieve that stake with the bet on the shorter priced selection.

If your two selections are at 4-1 and 5-2, put £25 to win on the former (to win £100) and £10 on the latter (to retrieve the £25 stake). If the longer priced selection wins, you win £90; if the shorter, you break even; and if both lose, you lose £35. If both are at the same price, aim to win £100 with each.

Assuming that wins and losses are *equally* distributed between shorter and longer priced selections, this is a way of maximising your winnings when a longer priced selection wins. You may think it very unlikely that you will be able to get 7-2 about a dog which you think has a very good chance; or even more unlikely that you can get better than 5-2 against 2 dogs which have very good chances. Here you must make a study of the betting market at the different courses.

I have given my views in the next chapter, but I do suggest that you study the markets carefully to identify the stronger markets which in your opinion offer value, and the weaker ones which do not.

Finally, a word on staking plans. Many racing systems seem to give more attention to complex staking plans which 'guarantee' large profits than to the mechanics of finding winners. I concentrate on finding winners, and generally bet on level stakes.

The only principle worth following is 'play up your winnings and cut your losses', and there are several quite simple methods of doing this. The one I recommend is that you set aside a bank of 100 units (say £200) and bet 10 units (in this case, £20), until you have doubled your bank. This is now 200 units (£400), and you should follow the same procedure until you double your bank again.

Another equally simple plan is sometimes called '10%' staking. You set aside a bank of 100 points, and add your winnings or deduct your losses after each bet. Every time you bet, you stake 10% of whatever the bank amounts to. For example, you start with a 10 points stake on your first bet. If your first bet is a loser, you have lost 10 points, and your bank is now 90 points, so you bet 10% of this on your second bet, ie 9 points. If you begin with a winner, say at 4-1, you add 40 points to your bank, so that for your second bet you stake 10% of 140 points, ie 14 points.

In the first staking plan, it may take you quite a time to double your bank, but this system will in the long run make the most of your winnings - and to get cleaned out, you would have to have 10 straight losers. If you followed my method carefully, and always looked for value for money, this would be quite an achievement. In the second staking plan, you can theoretically bet for ever, as your bank will never be totally exhausted. Whichever staking plan you choose, follow it systematically and rigorously and it will form a vital part of your betting strategy.

CHAPTER SEVEN

At the Tracks

Horse-racing enthusiasts familiar with the wide variety of British and Irish racecourses may see all greyhound tracks as alike. It is true that there is only one track with an uphill finish (Enniscorthy), but there are significant differences between the tracks which must be taken into account.

For the form student, the ideal track would be a big, wide, galloping circuit with a long run to the first bend; easy, well-banked turns; and a long run-in to the winning post.

This kind of layout gives a fair chance to all sorts of dogs, from the small, nippy type to the well-built galloper. The long run to the first gives the early paced dogs the opportunity to get clear of the slower starters, so that there isn't a pile up at the first bend; and the long run in gives the late finishers time and space to deliver their challenge.

Harringay was the classic track of this type. Although the closure of White City, the largest track in Britain, was a great loss to the sport, its relatively short run in did not give the late finisher much of a chance. Of the currently operating NGRC fully licensed tracks, 10 are of this kind - Brough Park, Hackney, Hall Green, Hove, Monmore Green, Nottingham, Shawfield, Sheffield (Owlerton), Swindon and Wembley. Of the leading permit tracks, Swaffham has a layout very much like that of the old Harringay track.

One difference between the tracks which I don't think significant is the hare type. In the McGee type (used at a minority of the tracks), the hare runs along a sunken channel; in the Sumner type it runs on a suspended arm. Nearly all the tracks now have an outside hare - but inside or outside, Sumner or McGee, it doesn't seem to make any difference to how the runners perform.

This chapter gives an appraisal of the leading tracks for which form details are given in the sporting press. In my opinion, the backer can find by far the best opportunities at : Hackney (484 and 523 metres), followed in order by : Hove (515 and 695 metres); Wembley (655 metres); Walthamstow (640 metres); and Monmore Green (484 metres).

If your local track is not dealt with here, you should apply the principles explained earlier in the book. In particular, you should compile an index of times for various grades; and target times for the sectionals in different grades. Unfortunately, this is not always possible, as many tracks do not have any form of sectional timing.

You should also find out what kind of running style is suited by the layout of the track. This cannot be done by guesswork based on your impressions after watching a number of races - it can only be done by *analysing* the results of a significant number of races. The following table, based on an analysis of the running style of the winners of 100 races at each track shows how different tracks can be.

Grading policy also differs at various tracks and if you follow racing consistently, this will readily become apparent. The grader does have to work with the material to hand, and the best way of calculating track strength is to work out how many multiple winners there are at each distance.

Winners by :	Early pace	Late finish
CRAYFORD ('M')	52%	16%
HACKNEY ('A' and 'M')	24%	26%
HOVE ('A')	43%	27%
HOVE ('S')	17%	24%
WALTHAMSTOW ('S')	10%	23%
WEMBLEY ('A')	59%	16%
WEMBLEY ('S')	46%	23%
WIMBLEDON ('S')	24%	13%

Again, there are quite considerable variations between the tracks. For example, over 515 metres at Hove, 100 races were won by just 44 dogs; whereas over 490 metres at Wembley, 72 dogs were involved. In my opinion, the tracks/distances which have more multiple winners favour the backer, as the results are more predictable.

Finally, the percentage of truly-run races varies quite considerably from track to track. For example, only about 30% of the 470 metre races at Bristol are trouble-free, while at Hackney over the 523 metres, the proportion is about 60%. Clearly, it makes more sense to look for tracks at which your selection is less likely to meet interference.

BRISTOL

This is quite a good galloping track, with a run up of 90 metres to the first bend, easy turns and a long enough run-in to allow a late challenge.

Since 1987, the number of higher grade races included in the BAGS programme has increased significantly. On the other hand, I suspect that the winner of an A1 here is not quite of the same standard as the top graded racers at other tracks.

There is an even distribution of winners from the traps, so that to be drawn in Trap 3 or Trap 4 does not seem to be as much of a handicap as it is elsewhere.

Unfortunately, to offset these positive features, there are two drawbacks. The standard 'A' distance of 470 metres is just a bit too short, which may be the cause of the fact that the proportion of reliable races is quite low (around 30%).

Secondly, in recent years, the betting market seems rather weak - it is difficult to get a good price if you do have a confident selection.

Grading-in 470 metres ('A') : 29.90 seconds

A3 = 29.30 = 100

BROUGH PARK

This is a very wide, galloping track, with a circumference of 415 metres and a run-in of over 80 metres - an ideal type in fact.

Unfortunately, on the BAGS programme it only offers lower grade racing, with the top grade being A4. Furthermore, an A4 here seems to be quite weak in comparison to an A4 at, say, Wembley. The evening programmes do offer some higher grade races, but also a large number of handicaps, popular with northern racegoers.

Grading-in 500 metres ('A') : 32.70 seconds

A5 = 31.90

CATFORD

The 333 metre circuit is the sharpest in Britain. However, the bends are well banked, and the handy well-balanced animal finds no problems in running the bends at speed. Early paced railers and bitches seem to do well, but, surprisingly enough, over the 555 metres distance, late finishers also have a respectable record. There is usually a competitive programme of higher grade racing here, but because of the nature of the track, I find it wiser not to bet.

If you like this track, I think you should concentrate on the 555 metre races ('A'). The 385 metres ('K') sprint is rather a mad dash; and form tends to be somewhat unreliable over the 718 metres ('S'), the longest regular distance for graded racers at any British track.

Grading-in 555 metres ('A') : 36.60 seconds

A3 = 35.80 = 100

A2 = 35.70 = 110

A1 = 35.50 = 120

CRAYFORD

The old track, with its circumference of 408 metres, was of reasonable size, but the new track is completely different. It is an object lesson in the economics of modern greyhound racing - the old track occupied 20 acres of ground, the new required only one-quarter the space. It has a circumference of 334 metres, with about 78 metres to the first bend, and a distance of only 380 metres in the 'A' grades. The bends are rather tight, with minimal banking.

Racing here is a lottery, more like canine bingo. In the 'A' grade races, unless your selection gets to the first bend in front, s/he might as well stay in the kennels. Even the 540 metre ('M') distance is rather sharp, and poses similar problems, but if you must bet here, it offers the least worst option.

To make the backer's task even harder, the betting market here rarely seems to offer value for money.

Grading-in 540 metres ('M') : 36.80 seconds

M3 = 35.45 = 100

M2 = 35.35 = 110

M1 = 35.10 = 135

HACKNEY

For the form enthusiast, this is as near perfection as you are likely to get. A good galloping circuit with a circumference of 436 metres which gives very reliable results; all the racing is on the BAGS programme; and a strong betting market, which gives good value for money - it's not surprising that Hackney is the favourite BAGS course of the majority of betting shop punters.

TYPES OF RACES

484 metres ('A') : the 81 metres to the first bend is a bit sharp, but the rest of

the circuit with its easy turns, long back straight, and generous run in, more than makes up for this minor shortcoming.

Over this distance, Traps 1 and 6 have a very definite advantage. Unless a dog has a considerable sectional time advantage over his rivals *and* a very good early pace for the grade, it is hard to win from Traps 3 and 4 by early speed.

523 metres ('M') : with its 120 metres run to the first bend, there are no faults over this distance. The long run to the first allows runners to sort themselves out, and there is rarely any serious bunching. My records show that over 60% of the races here provide a reliable result - the highest of any track and distance.

Because of the long run from the traps, trap position is relatively unimportant. However, I would expect a dog in Traps 3 or 4 to have won from these traps in the past.

INDEX FIGURES AND TARGET SECTIONALS

A3 = 30.20 = 100   3.95

A2 = 30.15 = 105   3.90

A1 = 30.00 = 120   3.85

M3 = 32.60 = 100   6.00

M2 = 32.40 = 120   5.95

M1 = 32.35 = 125   5.90

HALL GREEN

The long straights and well banked bends ensure a good gallop and trouble-free races. There is quite a long run-in (over 65 metres) giving the late-finishing type every chance. Races over 663 metres ('S') are a very searching test, as the traps are placed virtually at the end of the back straight. The graded racing here is of good quality : the only drawback is that the card usually has 2 or 3 handicap races.

Grading-in 474 metres ('A') : 30.00 seconds; 663 metres ('S') : 43.10 seconds.

HOVE

The only grass track on the BAGS circuit, though how much longer it will remain unsanded is questionable. Time variations can be considerable during a hard winter, but in the summer it seems to be fairly consistent.

This is a big galloping circuit, with long swinging bends, and a circumference of 455 metres. It has flourishing local support, so the BAGS programme usually includes only the lower grade racing. Do not be misled by the grading titles - an A5 here is the equivalent of an A3 or even an A2 at many other tracks. I have not found enough graded races titled A2 and A1 here to compile figures.

Hove also stages races limited to puppies, marked by the prefix 'P'. This seems fairer on the puppies, but I still avoid these races. Although they won't get bumped by their seniors, they are still likely to run inconsistently from the traps.

Hove is a very good example of the fluctuations of a track's fortunes. In 1987 and 1988 there were very few graded races above A3 or S3, so the time figures for these grades are not available. Towards the end of 1988 there was a noticeable improvement in the quality of the dogs on the kennel strength, leading to a considerable increase in the number of higher graded races.

Ideal in other respects, as the betting market is quite reasonable, unfortunately the BAGS programme here includes little A3 equivalent racing, which is reserved for the evening patrons.

TYPES OF RACES

515 metres ('A') : like Hackney, the run to the first bend is on the sharp side (81 metres), but this is followed by very wide swinging bends, and enough of a run in to allow a late challenge.

Traps 1 and 6 have definite advantages, but wide runners can sometimes go really adrift on these very long bends.

695 metres ('S') : this is a really testing distance once the dogs get going, and late finishers have a good record over this trip. Because the traps are set only 35 metres from the first bend, early paced dogs find it difficult to slip their field, and have a relatively poor record.

Grading-in 515 metres ('A') : 31.90 seconds; 695 metres ('S') 43.80 seconds

INDEX FIGURES

A5 = 31.20 = 100

A4 = 31.10 = 110

A3 = 31.00 = 120

S3 = 43.00 = 100

MONMORE GREEN

One of the widest racing circuits in Britain (7 metres), this is a big galloping course (circumference 416 metres), with a good run in.

The best racing takes place in the evening programme, as the BAGS programme is usually made up of 8 runner handicaps or lower grade races over the 484 course, neither of which offer us any opportunities.

Given the difficulties of finding a winner in the 8 runner handicaps, the betting market seems rather cramped, but offers reasonable value in the other types of races.

462 metres ('A') : although there is a good run to the first bend of 92 metres, I find the overall distance too short - it does not allow any margin for recovery. Consequently I never bet in these races.

484 metres ('M') : the wide and long run to the first bend (114 metres) gives the field plenty of time to sort itself out. The rest of the circuit offers every type of dog a chance, and generally provides reliable results with a high proportion of multiple winners. This distance seems to favour wide runners, and dogs drawn in the outside traps have a definite advantage. Because of the width of the track, the late finisher has plenty of space for a challenge, and this type of dog is particularly suited to the course.

647 metres ('5'): this is a good test of stamina, with its run-up of 67 metres to the first bend. Unfortunately, ordinary graded races are rarely run over this distance, which is reserved for handicaps.

Grading-in 484 metres ('A') : 31.50 seconds; 647 metres ('5') 43.70seconds.

INDEX FIGURES

M3 = 30.40 = 100

ROMFORD

This is a tight circuit, with a circumference of 350 metres. In the 'A' grades (400m) there is only 67 metres to the first bend, so that Trap 1 is unduly favoured. The 575m has a similarly short run to the first bend, but over this longer trip it is worth looking for a bitch in form which has won at the track - bitches seem to adapt well to this tricky circuit. Course specialists are favoured here, as at Catford, but in my opinion it is very difficult to find winners here.

Grading-in 575 metres ('M') : 37.40 seconds

WALTHAMSTOW

Like Hove, this is a grass track, but with sanded bends throughout the year. With a circumference of 405 metres, the straights are long, but the bends are rather tight and not as well banked as at some other tracks. There is always a considerable amount of baulking and bumping at the bends, more than in any of the tracks reviewed in this chapter. This makes for a low proportion (about 25%) of reliable results.

This is rather a pity, as there is always a good programme of competitive higher graded races, with at least 3 such races on every card. Walthamstow's popularity has increased greatly in recent years, and its Tote turnover is the highest of all tracks. Nonetheless, the betting market is strong, and value for money is always available.

TYPES OF RACES

475 metres ('A') : there is a long run to the first bend, of 100 metres, but this is offset by the sharp bends - much of the scrimmaging takes place at this bend. The run in to the winning post is over 70 metres, and although this is not a wide track, the late finisher has every chance.

Trap 6 is the best Trap at this distance, as wide runners in this trap and all the trouble. The type of dog to look for at this track is the handy late finisher running from Trap 6.

640 metres ('S') : the run to the first bend is 68 metres, but there is as much bumping at this distance as over the shorter trip. A dog which can be relied in to put in a clear round often has a better chance than faster rivals which tend to run into trouble. Late finishers have a good record here, and the trap position is not quite as crucial as it is over the shorter distance. Early-paced dogs have the poorest record (10% of winners) of any track reviewed in this chapter.

Grading-in 475 metres ('A') : 30.10 seconds; 640 metres ('S') : 41.10 seconds

INDEX FIGURES

** At this track, you should constantly monitor the recorded times, as at the seasonal change over the extent of the track which is sanded changes, giving rise to significant time variations.

A3 = 29.35 = 100

A2 = 29.25 = 110

A1 = 28.95 = 140

S3 = 40.80 = 100

S2 = 40.50 = 130
S1 = 40.45 = 135

WEMBLEY

With a circumference of 435 metres (third only to Hackney and Hove of the courses analysed here), this is an excellent galloping track, testing stamina to the full. However, it does have two negative aspects : unlike most tracks, the bends are not banked; and the straights are rather narrow (4m).

The quality of graded racing here is very high - an A1 here is often of much better quality than some Open Races at other tracks. Unfortunately, racing is due to numerous interruptions from the other events (pop concerts etc) staged at the stadium, particularly during the summer months. Continuity of form is therefore often lacking.

The grader has plenty of good dogs to choose from, and I find the graded races very difficult to solve. I get the impression that the grader is rather severe on winners in the lower grades. Double-grading for winners which have not recorded particularly fast times seems quite common.

Until quite recently, Wembley was the only British track which employed true sectional timing - ie the time to the first bend. Unfortunately, it has now reverted to a sectional recorded at the winning post.

If you find a dog with a very good chance, the betting market is very open and surprisingly good value is often available.

TYPES OF RACES

490 metres ('A') : there is a good run to the first bend, of 95 metres, and early paced dogs have a tremendous record over this distance - the highest proportion (59%) of all the leading tracks. The type you should look for is the big (over, say, 34 kgs) early-paced dog which can set up a tremendous gallop from the start. Late-finishers have a poor record.

However, it can be difficult to find winners here. Because of the track strength and the grader's policy, races are evenly distributed over a large number of dogs, more so than at any other track for which I have calculated the results.

655 metres ('S') : this is an excellent test of stamina, and provides a good proportion of cleanly run races. Winners are much easier to find than over the shorter distance - although the early-paced types do very well (46% of winners), the late finishers have a much better chance (23%) than over 490 metres.

Because this is such a searching test of stamina, there are far more multiple winners than over the shorter distance. Consequently, the grader tends to handicap winners by putting them into 490 metre races. Winners return to their grade over this distance much more quickly than they do in the 'A' races.

INDEX FIGURES

A3 = 29.80 = 100
A2 = 29.70 = 110
A1 = 29.60 = 120
S3 = 40.90 = 100
S2 = 40.75 = 115
S1 = 40.60 = 140

WIMBLEDON

This is a reasonable sized track, with a circumference of 408 metres. Its 120 metres run to the first bend should make for reliable results even given the shortness of the 'A' races, 460 metres, but the sharp turn cancels out these advantages. Many dogs lose their chances completely at this point, and even the long run in does not offer a chance of recovery.

Even the extra 20 metres to the 480 metres winning post of the Derby does not seem to help. This course definitely favours the handily built runner at the expense of the big galloping type - it does seem unreasonable that the prestige event of the season should be run here.

The betting market is strong, and value for money is easy to find.

TYPES OF RACES

460 and 480 metres ('A') : for the reasons given above, I do not follow these races.

660 metres ('S') : this is quite a different matter - for our purposes, this is the best of the 'S' distance races at the tracks analysed in this chapter. The 120 metres run to the first bend, followed by a relatively easy turn, means that a good dog can easily steer clear of trouble. By the time they reach the first bend of the 460 track, the field is usually well separated. However, for no apparent reason, the results are seldom clear cut.

Because of the long opening run, to be drawn in Traps 3 and 4 does not seem an insuperable disadvantage. Even so, I prefer a Trap 4 dog to have won previously from this trap.

Grading-in 660 metres ('S') : 41.80 seconds

INDEX FIGURES

S3 = 41.80 = 100

CHAPTER EIGHT

Ten Golden Rules

1. Always base your selections on recent winning form - ideally, a win in the same grade within the last 30 days.

2. Never back a greyhound only because it has recorded a faster time than any of the other dogs in the race. Your selection must have recorded a good time for the grade. Never back a dog to win in a higher grade in which it has not previously won.

3. Look for a good racing style : either early pace or a strong late finish. Avoid the 'chasers', the 'faders' and those which do not have a clear-cut winning style.

4. Never back a puppy, that is, a greyhound less than two years old.

5. Be wary of backing an older greyhound, that is, older than three years six months. You should certainly not back a greyhound which wins by early pace, when it is over three years old.

6. Always back bitches which show winning form 16-20 weeks after their seasonal date, provided that they have recorded a faster time than any of the other competitors last time out, and they have recorded an index figure of more than 50.

7. Choose a track and racing distance which allow all types of dogs an equal chance, and which give a high proportion of reliable results.

8. Always go to the track to see whether your selection is fully fit and ready to win.

9. Always bet methodically : start with a bank; follow a staking plan; and keep a record of all your bets.

10. Be patient and wait until everything is in your favour. In terms of your betting strategy you should bet on the course (when there is no tax), in single, win only bets. Always aim to get 3-1 or better for graded races; and 2-1 or better for Open Races. If you must take shorter prices, never ever bet odds on.